Emerson, Our Contemporary

Emerson, Our

Crowell-Collier Press • Collier-Macmillan Limited, London

Contemporary

August Derleth

Grateful acknowledgment is made to Houghton Mifflin Company, as the authorized publishers of the works of Ralph Waldo Emerson, for permission to quote at will from *The Complete Works of Ralph Waldo Emerson* as well as *The Journals of Ralph Waldo Emerson,* and to the Ralph Waldo Emerson Memorial Association and Columbia University Press for permission to quote at discretion from *The Letters of Ralph Waldo Emerson,* edited by Ralph L. Rusk.

Photograph courtesy of The Bettmann Archive

Contents

Stripped of its idealistic phraseology, of its beauty and fervor, the master idea of the Emersonian philosophy is the divine sufficiency of the individual.
                    —Vernon L. Parrington,
          Main Currents in American Thought

At the time of his death in 1882 Ralph Waldo Emerson was widely regarded as the most distinguished and most influential of American authors. He had spent a lifetime fighting the rising tide of materialism, serenely and with the utmost self-confidence. He was an idealist who nevertheless saw reality with cold, clear eyes, and never faltered in his pursuit of truth. He condemned materialism but at the same time he turned his back upon the ministry for which he had been educated and confessed himself dissatisfied with the spiritual life of his age.

He was a Jeffersonian in that he looked with disfavor on the growing industrialism that was altering the face and character of his country and expressed a marked preference for an agrarian order. Like his neighbor and friend, Henry Thoreau, he preferred simplicity but, unlike him, he found it possible to compromise between the ideal and the reality, however severe he was in refusing any compromise in his search for truth, which he conducted with a Spartan honesty and a dedicated patience.

Emerson's essays remain today among the best prose set down by American writers. His work continues to appear in American textbooks, and the best of it has been kept in print since his death. Though himself an indifferent poet, the poetic

Foreword

tradition he inaugurated has flourished and come to full flower in our own time.

"To believe your own thought, to believe that what is true for you in your private heart, is true for all men—that is genius," he wrote in his essay, *Self-Reliance*. That genius Ralph Waldo Emerson never betrayed.

Emerson, Our Contemporary

*The purpose of life seems to be to acquaint
a man with himself. He is not to live to the
future as described to him, but to live to the
real future by living to the real present.
The highest revelation is that God is in
every man.*
    The Journals of Ralph Waldo Emerson

Ralph Waldo Emerson was born in Boston on May 25, 1803, the third son of William and Ruth Haskins Emerson. His father was a moderately successful Unitarian minister of uncertain health. Before he was three years old, Ralph was going to the equivalent of a kindergarten school; he set no high marks there as a young scholar, perhaps not unnaturally, and was accounted rather dull.

What he remembered of his childhood, apart from the delight he took in his home, was summed up in the hymns his father taught him to memorize, the curative baths his father forced him to take, and the severity of one of his teachers, Lawson Lyon. His aunt Mary Moody Emerson loomed largest on his horizon outside the family circle. She was an opinionated, contradictory spinster devoted to ideas, and constantly urged her young nephew to scorn trifles and lift his aims; being somewhat unconventional herself, she adjured him to "do what you are afraid to do."

In common with the children of other ministers, he was much exposed to clergymen and Christian precepts. Sunday in the Emerson household began with Saturday evening, and was a day of more than ordinary religious observance—and ordinary weekdays had their share of family prayers and

CHAPTER 1

The Early Years

Scripture readings. Since more than one of his forebears were ministers, Ralph was early inclined toward the ministry as a career.

The security of the household was shaken with the death of his father on May 12, 1811. At eight, Ralph walked with his brother William behind the coffin in the long cortege that bore his father's body away, not as much moved by the solemnity of the occasion as impressed by the pomp of the procession.

Though the First Church permitted the widow Emerson to live for a while in the rectory, and to continue to receive the stipend paid to her husband as salary, it was clear that changes would have to be made. Ralph's brother Bulkeley was sent to live with relatives in Maine, and his brother Edward went to live in Concord with his grandfather Ezra Ripley, who had married his grandmother, Phebe Bliss Emerson, after the death of his grandfather William Emerson. There Ralph joined Edward that summer, after the auction of his father's library in August. Mary Moody Emerson came to lend a hand in the household.

At nine, Ralph was old enough to enter the Boston Public Latin School, which was primitive in structure and administration. He spent some time also at the South Writing School on West Street, and frequently yielded to the temptation to play truant when on his way from one school to the other, not much deterred by the knowledge of inevitable punishment, for the Boston Common and the city's wharves proved considerably more stimulating to his imagination than the school sessions.

Soon, too, he was trying his hand at verse. Not unexpectedly, he turned to celebration of the Sabbath, writing seven stanzas of lines like

4

> Remember your Redeemer's love,
> And meditate on things above,
> Forsake while you are here below,
> The path which leads to realms of woe.

advocating church attendance and prayer. Neither this nor other early verses ever appeared in any collection bearing his name.

From religious subjects, the budding poet turned to patriotism, inspired by events of the War of 1812. He celebrated the Battle of Lake Erie in *Perry's Victory*, part of which reads as follows:

> When late Columbia's patriot brave
> Sail'd forth on Erie's tranquil wave
> No hero yet had found a grave—
> Within her watery cemetery.
> But soon that wave was stained with gore
> And soon as every concave shore
> Re-echoed with the dreadful roar
> Of thundering artillery.

He also celebrated military events apart from his own country's, particularly the Russians' defeat of Napoleon. He wrote nonsense verses, took to writing letters in verse, wrote elegies, and put together pages of octosyllabic couplets which he called *The History of Fortus*.

His chief mentor was none of his teachers, but his aunt Mary Moody Emerson. Second to her was her friend Sarah Alden Bradford, with whom the lad carried on a faithful correspondence; she encouraged his bent toward versifying, and to her he wrote many letters in verse, some of them about ancient history and the Greek and Roman classics.

In 1814, circumstances combined to effect major changes in the household at the Summer Street rectory. Rising prices had already impelled Mrs. Emerson to take boarders, of whom the first was, quite naturally, the new pastor. The war seemed from time to time to threaten Boston, and the widow began to look for lodgings elsewhere.

In that year her only surviving daughter, three-year-old Mary Caroline, sickened and died, leaving Mrs. Emerson with but the five sons—William, Ralph, Edward, Charles, and the mentally retarded Bulkeley. Before the year was out, in October, Mrs. Emerson's father, John Haskins, also died.

By this time the Emerson household was making plans to move to Concord. Boston was under blockade, and Concord seemed a safer haven. Early in November the move was made, and Ralph found himself with his family established in the home of his paternal grandmother Phebe Bliss Ripley and grandfather, Ezra Ripley. He was no stranger to the Old Manse, for he had visited there in the summers, and Concord exactly suited him.

Indeed, Concord must have seemed to him almost more of a native place—it was his father's—than Boston, for Concord had been the home of his ancestors for several generations. During almost a century and a half, the clergymen of Concord had been Ralph's ancestors, and in 1814 Concord was central to Emerson family relationships, for almost all Ralph's relatives lived within fifty miles of Concord.

His new home gave Ralph more freedom. Here he need not walk the streets in fear of the rough bullies from Windmill Point and the South End who were always ready to pick fights with the West End lads. Here he could go abroad with his grandfather and hear the lore and history of Concord from the old man. Best of all, in Concord he was face to face with nature, and he took joy in its aspects, in the Concord River that flowed behind the Old Manse, in the Sudbury and Assabet rivers that formed the Concord River, and the meadows and marshes adjacent to them. He had his tasks, but carrying water and wood, and keeping the fireplace or shoveling snow, did not detract at all from the charm of Concord.

Nor did school, which he soon told his correspondents he liked better every day.

He wrote verses more diligently than ever. More, he occasionally mounted a sugar barrel in Deacon White's store and declaimed his verses aloud. His lines were stiff and often labored. He saluted George Washington and peace; he continued to write patriotic couplets about his country.

But the Concord sojourn was not destined to last long. With the end of the War of 1812, Mrs. Emerson looked again to Boston for some means to alleviate the family's poverty. Uncertainly as she viewed taking in boarders, she saw no other course open to her. By the spring the family was back in Boston—at first with the Haskins family, but presently with the Daniel Parkers on Beacon Street. There was one less mouth to feed, for William had gone off to college with a grant from the First Church to aid him in his education.

The disciplines of poverty and religion honed young Ralph. If the countryside was no longer as accessible to him, there was no dearth of books. He read voraciously in school and out. He wrote voluminously, turning ever and anon to irony, whimsy, satire. He studied French. Back in Latin School, his headmaster, Benjamin Apthorp Gould, encouraged him in speech and stimulated his writing. Gould permitted him to read his verses now and then when an appropriate program presented itself.

If he carried off no honors from the Latin School, he did occasionally win plaudits from his audience. Gould taxed his more promising students with themes and poems. Ralph formed an affinity for Samuel Johnson. He enjoyed history, even geography, but, like so many students who excel in English, he disliked mathematics.

The Latin School was not alone in contributing to his knowledge. He took books from the Boston Library Society. He read fiction, drama, poetry, philosophy. He read Walter Scott, Goldsmith, the *Arabian Nights,* Cicero, Maria Edgeworth, Chaucer, and many others.

Quite possibly his family's removal from the Parker house on Beacon Street to another home on Hancock Street had little meaning for Ralph, whose exploration of the mind's country now took precedence over all else. With William gone, Ralph was Mrs. Emerson's oldest son at home, and she leaned on him to carry out household obligations as well as to keep her company though Ralph was no longer inclined— as in his early school years—to ignore his studies. Aunt Mary Emerson was, as usual, here and gone; when she was in residence with the Emersons, she was—despite a certain forthright cantankerousness—of great help to Ruth Emerson, and a goad for the Emerson children, who were enriched by her tart observations on life and manners, and confirmed in their faith by her unswerving devotion to the Bible.

From Hancock Street to Essex Street was the next move for the Emersons. There Ruth Emerson continued to take in boarders and tried to see her way clear to send Ralph to college.

In July of 1817 the First Church assigned to Ralph the same grant that his brother William had received; it was no secret that Ralph was bound for college, whatever the financial difficulties of the Emerson family. Gould advised him not to delay going to college, but to leave that Fall, and by college he meant Harvard. Indeed, any other college was unthinkable.

Early one September morning he walked to Cambridge so that he could be there by six o'clock and present himself for the entrance examination, which he passed with distinction.

*The things taught in colleges and schools
are not an education, but the means of
education.*
The Journals of Ralph Waldo Emerson

A t Harvard, Emerson was appointed orderly to President John Thornton Kirkland and given a room in the rear of Wadsworth House beneath the president's study. As a student in a quasi-official position, he was not charged for a study but he had to pay the customary tuition fee. He managed to make fifty dollars or less do for every quarter's expenses, which included everything from tuition to a fee for firewood. He may have chafed a little at having to help enforce the strict rules of the college, which was one of the obligations of the president's orderly, but he did not fail his duties.

He was now in his fifteenth year, somewhat younger than average for his class; but he was taller than average, and his demeanor was grave and taciturn, out of a kind of dignity that came naturally to him, one that, nevertheless, concealed some uncertainty and shyness.

Solitude became the poet in him and he was much alone. He had comparatively few friends, though he walked about Cambridge with his old Summer Street neighbor and schoolmate, John Gardner, who later recalled that Ralph was "not talkative . . . but there was a certain flash when he uttered anything more than usually worthy to be remembered." He

CHAPTER 2

Harvard and the Ministry

took little part in class activities, though he wrote a song for a freshman dinner that followed an examination, and heard it sung.

His dislike of mathematics continued. He had difficulty with the subject, despite some assistance from Gould, his Latin School headmaster. He refused, however, to worry about it, wrestle as he might with the complexities of numbers, and before his freshman year was done he had convinced himself that it was not necessary to understand mathematics—he added Greek—"to be a good, useful, or even *great* man." Despite his relative dislike of Greek, he was considerably more at ease with it than with mathematics. And, though he hated mathematics, for a time early in his freshman year he tutored President Kirkland's nephew, Samuel Lothrop, in arithmetic, among other subjects.

He was devoted to the study of history and biography, and his curiosity about these subjects did not abate throughout his lifetime. He was also much given to declamations, which were a weekly feature and went far to preparing him to preach and lecture.

During the winter and spring holidays Ralph taught a class of fourteen at his uncle Samuel Ripley's school in Waltham. William had done so before him and Edward would also teach in that school. Ralph had not yet reached his fifteenth birthday.

He was a little more sure of himself in his sophomore year. With a classmate, William Bradley Dorr, he stayed at room 5 in Hollis Hall, within view of the Cambridge Common. He saw Dorr as a waggish and rather mischievous fellow; perhaps Dorr contributed to a somewhat increased gregariousness on Emerson's part. He found himself oftener among his classmates and even, on one occasion when over a score of sophomores had rebelled against the disciplines and were suspended, remained at home for some time out of loyalty to them. His absence, however, was not punished; he was given a position as waiter when he returned.

Nevertheless, he was not particularly a joiner, describing himself as "a spectator rather than a fellow." He stayed clear of such popular clubs as the Porcellian, the Order of Knights of the Square Table, and Hasty Pudding. He avoided also most of the religious societies, though he was active in the Adelphoi Theologia, and he was a member of some lesser, more intimate clubs, given to study and conviviality. Before his sophomore year was done, he was elected to the Pythologian Club, which pleased him because its membership included "the fifteen smartest fellows in each of the two classes Junior & Soph."

The expenses of going to college were a recurrent subject in his letters to his brothers, William and Edward, though his circumstances in his sophomore year in this respect were improved over those of his freshman year. He still retained the First Church grant, known as the Penn legacy. In February, 1819, he wrote to William about his appointment as a waiter in the junior commons: "I am to wait in the Junior Hall; I do like it & yet I do not like it." By April 1 he wrote that he was finally to receive some of the benefit of the legacy left by Mary Saltonstall in 1730, to be used "for the assistance of two persons who shall by the overseers be esteemed of bright parts & good diligence (allways a Dissenter) to fit them for the Service of the Church of Christ," when he explained "the Prest [sic] was very gracious—told me I had grown & said he hoped *intellectually* as well as *physically* & told me (better than all) when my next bill comes out to bring it to him as I had never received the Saltonstall benefit promised me before I entered College. My next bill had not come out yet but I think I shall be inclined to remember *that*."

His studies put no limitations upon his poetizing. Declamation and composition were part of his curriculum. However

13

much he hated mathematics—and he made no secret of this, setting it forth bluntly in his letters to his brother William— he studied algebra and geometry. In Greek he had been "taken up every time," but his "criticism [a theme] on Guillaume le Conqurant [sic] had two marks on the back, which distinction only six of the class obtained." He toyed with the idea of competing for the Bowdoin prize, given annually at Harvard; "I am very doubtful about writing this year," he wrote William, "for though reading Boswell I have not read half of Johnson's works; & probably a great many will try for it." He thought he would "do better to be a year writing the Character of Socrates" *(A Dissertation on the Character of Socrates)*. He confessed himself enamored of logic, and much taken with philosophy, but he was not pleased with the subjects assigned for rhetoric. Study as he might—and he applied himself industriously—he found time to compose poems.

Most of his poetry in his college years lacked distinction. He wrote largely derivative, imitative verse, reflecting the melancholy of so much verse of his day as well as the sensibility of the age. But he also composed drinking songs and heard them sung by the clubs to which he belonged.

In his junior year, he was much impressed by Professor Edward Everett, who had come back from abroad to resume his teaching. His eloquent lectures readily found an appreciative listener in one who, since he was aiming for the ministry, was naturally inclined toward the swelling eloquence of sermons. At the same time, he came under the instruction of Edward Tyrrel Channing in rhetoric and oratory. Both men helped to increase Emerson's admiration for Greek and Greece, and his reading for the Bowdoin prize essay helped to clarify his understanding of Greek thought.

But perhaps none of his teachers influenced him as much as George Ticknor, whose lectures in French literature led him to what he was soon describing as the "most extraordinary" book every written—the essays of Montaigne, his enthusiasm for which was to grow.

He had for some time been keeping a journal—perhaps since his matriculation at Harvard, though the earliest journal to survive goes back no further than 1820; since he numbered it XVII, an earlier date for the beginning of his journal must be presumed. He needed some outlet for his thoughts, some repository for the impressions that crowded upon him. He called his journal a diary at first, named it his "Blotting-Book" and "Wide World" and "Common Place book." He wrote under date of January 25, 1820, "These pages are intended at their commencement to, contain a record of new thoughts (when they occur); for a receptacle of all the old ideas that partial but peculiar peepings at antiquity can furnish or furbish; for tablet to save the wear and tear of weak Memory, and, in short, for all the various purposes and utility, real or imaginary, which are usually comprehended under that comprehensive title *Common Place book*."

He did not at first write much in it. His notebooks, kept in Ticknor's class, were far more elaborate. He set down a "character" of Daniel Webster published by "a lawyer of Boston," evidently in a lecture. In March he confessed that he had "been better employed" than at writing in his journal, by which he meant that he was, as usual, writing prose, poetry, and "miscellany," not to mention reading for his essay to be entered for the Bowdoin Prize.

From time to time fragments of original verse appeared in his journal as well as copies of lines that pleased him, drafts of essays, copies of letters, at least a few pages of an imaginative romance he evidently planned to write but never did, many paragraphs about literary subjects, chiefly imitative of the work of other authors—all matters belonging to his months

15

of study. Entries extraneous to his own thoughts largely vanished from the journal after he was graduated from Harvard in 1821, by which time he had behind him two second-place Bowdoin prizes—one for *A Dissertation on the Character of Socrates,* a second for his *Dissertation on the Present State of Ethical Philosophy.* He also had the distinction of being one of the few Boylston contestants whose orations were best, winning one of three second prizes.

Uncertain as he was from time to time, in regard to his future, nourishing, as he put it, "brilliant visions of future grandeur," he still saw the ministry as his goal. "I must prepare myself for the great profession I have purposed to undertake," he wrote in his journal in 1821. "I am to give my soul to God."

He was not destined for the immediate achievement of that goal, however. What loomed ahead was schoolteaching under his brother William, at William's school for young ladies. He did not view teaching with pleasure, particularly in his brother's school. He referred to teaching, in a letter to his Aunt Mary, as a "fatal Gehenna," and had some fear that teaching would diminish his impulse and ability to write poetry. Perhaps it did affect the entries in his journal, for he wrote nothing in it for months during the latter half of 1821.

By January 12, 1822, he turned to his journal again. "After a considerable interval I am still willing to think that these commonplace books are very useful and harmless things,—at least sufficiently so, to warrant another trial." Presumably he had made some adjustment to teaching and learned to take in stride the frustrations and vexations of the profession. He was only eighteen and too shy and uncertain of himself to enforce the disciplines of the school room. He referred to himself as "a hopeless Schoolmaster" and to teaching as "this miserable employment," and in one of his notebooks he put down the popular saying, "It takes philosopher or fool / to build a fire or keep a school."

Nevertheless, he was not bound to a desk, not prisoned by the obligations of teaching, and the topics he assigned to his students did not keep him into the midnight hours reading and correcting papers. He was able to find time to read and to write. In the late spring of 1822, he went on a walking tour with his brother William, to Northborough, some thirty miles away; there they were joined by Edward, who remained for a few days, after which Ralph walked with him to Worcester and so they parted. Ralph and William, staying in a farm-house near a pond, frequently lost themselves in the woods on the far shore, carrying books along to read as they stretched out in some sunny place. Sometimes Ralph fished but for the most part he vegetated.

"We passed our time in a manner exceedingly pleasant," he wrote to his aunt Mary Moody Emerson on June 10, "and drank as deeply of those delights for which Vertumnus is celebrated, as might be permitted to degraded uninitiated cits. I cannot tell, but it seemed to me that Cambridge would be a better place to study than the woodlands. I thought I under-stood a little of that *intoxication,* which you have spoken of; but its tendency was directly opposed to the slightest effort of mind or body; it was a soft animal luxury, the combined result of the beauty which fed the eye; the exhilarating Para-dise *air,* which fanned & dilated the sense; the novel melody, which warbled from the trees. Its first charm passed away rapidly with a longer acquaintance, but not once, during our stay, was I in any fit mood to take my pen, 'and rattle out the battles of my thoughts,' as Ben Jonson saith well. We dwelt near a pond which bore the name of 'Little Chauncey,' and often crossed it in a boat, then tied our bark to a tree on the opposite shore and plunged into the pathless woods, into forests silent since the birth of time, and lounged on the grass, with Bacon's Essays, or Milton, for hours. Perhaps in the Autumn, which I hold to be the finest season of the year, and in a longer abode the mind might, as you term it, return upon itself. . . ."

As time went on, the thoughts that occupied him lent themselves less readily to verse. He wrote less poetry, and began to consider the essay as a form in which to express himself. The moral sense, the problem of evil, the structure of the medieval church, modern Christianity, the lessons of history—these were the subjects that occupied his mind. He wrote a treatise called *Moral Obligation* and another titled *Thoughts on the Religion of the Middle Ages,* which became his first published piece, appearing in 1822 in the November and December issues of *The Christian Disciple.* He did not sign it, but used the initials H. O. N.

He continued to teach, however much he disliked it. In the summer of 1823 he and William had to walk two miles along the Dedham Turnpike to reach the school, for Ruth Emerson had moved her family once again, this time to the Canterbury area of Roxbury. The walk increased his delight in nature, as did his summer tours. That summer he walked to the Connecticut Valley as far afield as Northampton, once more with Bacon's essays for company.

Before the family was well settled on the Stedman Williams farm near Roxbury that May, Ralph and William signed a "declaration of faith" that made them members of the First Church in Boston, and before that summer had gone, Ralph had got into the habit of walking into Boston on Sundays to hear William Ellery Channing preach. His ambition to become a minister was fed and his inclination toward the ministry grew. Yet it was William who went abroad to study for the ministry, and Ralph and Edward who remained at home to teach school.

William's absence in no way diminished either Ralph's dislike of teaching or his ambition to enter the ministry. He was beginning to reach toward the central theme of all his thoughts, the theme around which all his thoughts were to become ordered—his belief in self-reliance. "Every wise man," he wrote in his journal, "aims at an entire conquest of himself."

He knew he must rely upon himself alone for his success; and if this were true for him, then certainly it was universally true. He was on more certain ground here than in his concern with nature and the concept of religion, for there was no way of knowing that any system of religion was true. When he contemplated his fellow-creatures other than man, he could not help reflecting that "he who has the same organization and a little more mind pretends to an insulated and extraordinary destiny to which his fellows of the stall and field are in no part admitted, nay are disdainfully excluded."

For all his slow formulation of the doctrine of self-reliance, he was not yet by any means self-assured. In 1824 he could write in his journal, "I cannot accurately estimate my chances of success, in my profession, and in life. Were it just to judge the future from the past, they would be very low. In my case, I think it is not. My trust is that my profession shall be my regeneration"—even if, as he also wrote, "Envy is the tax which all distinction must pay." William's letters home were not calculated to make Ralph's resolutions more firm, for his meetings with Goethe had brought him face to face with Goethe's belief that one's highest aim in life ought to be to "accommodate himself as perfectly as possible to the station in which he was placed."

Early in 1825 Ralph closed the school he had taken over from William when William went abroad, reckoning that he had earned two or three thousand dollars since leaving college, "which have paid my debts and obligated my neighbors." In February he returned to Harvard, entering the Divinity School, "grown closer," as he wrote in his journal, and with some knowledge "of the vanity of existence" and of "what shallow things men are, and how independent of external circumstances may be the states of mind called good and ill."

But his months of study were to be broken, his fortitude severely taxed. Family troubles abounded—Bulkeley's condition worsened, Edward suffered a breakdown and was forced to close his school, Ralph himself had trouble with his eyes and found it necessary to go back to teaching at Roxbury, then at Cambridge. William returned from study abroad and confessed that his mind was filled with doubt, which disturbed Ralph.

He wrote little in his journal; beset by the family troubles, he thought more and more often of another theme to which he was destined to return again and again. "All things are double one against another, said Solomon," he set down in his journal. "The whole of what we know is a system of compensations. Every defect in one manner is made up in another. Every suffering is rewarded; every sacrifice is made up; every debt is paid."

He concerned himself with faith, with the nature of friendship, made mockery of his ambition; he walked less because of a pain in his hip but he read more. The fact that he was so far from the realization of his ambition troubled him. "I confess the foolish ambition to be valued, with qualification. I do not want to be known by them that know me not, but where my name is mentioned I would have it respected."

He had grave periods of self-doubt, despite his growing conviction of self-reliance. He feared he would not live long enough to fulfill himself, to reach his goals, though he had as yet no very sure view of them, other than entering the ministry. He took a jaundiced view of his past. "My recollections of early life are not very pleasant."

In the summer of 1826 he found the text of his first sermon, which he titled *Pray Without Ceasing,* and set down its opening lines: "It is the duty of men to judge men only by their actions. Our faculties furnish us with no means of arriving at the motive, the character, the secret self." On October 10 of that year he delivered the sermon to the Middlesex Association.

"We call the tree good from its fruits, and the man, from his works," he declared. By this "work" the Middlesex Association judged him favorably. He was given his license to preach.

On October 15, he delivered his sermon to his uncle Samuel Ripley's congregation at Waltham, ascending the pulpit in a church for the first time as a preacher. And before that month had run its course, he closed his Cambridge school; it was his last venture into teaching.

Every promise of the soul has innumerable fulfilments; each of its joys ripens into a new want. Nature, uncontainable, flowing, forelooking, in the first sentiment of kindness anticipates already a benevolence which shall lose all particular regards in its general light. The introduction to this felicity is in a private and tender relation of one to one, which is the enchantment of human life; which, like a certain divine rage and enthusiasm, seizes on man at one period and works a revolution in his mind and body; unites him to his race, pledges him to the domestic and civic relations, carries him with new sympathy into nature, enhances the power of the senses, opens the imagination, adds to his character heroic and sacred attributes, establishes marriage and gives permanence to human society.

Love

Now, on the threshold of his career as a preacher, his health failed him again. His eyes improved but this time his lungs showed some symptoms of disease. His uncle Samuel Ripley lent him seventy dollars and urged him to take a voyage south for his health. Late in November, 1826, he took passage on the *Clematis,* bound for Charleston.

He spent the early months of 1827 in the south, going as far as St. Augustine, then returning to Charleston. In Charleston he was struck by southern manners and set forth in his journal: "Two negroes recognize each other in the street, though both in rags, and both it may be, balancing a burden on their heads, with the same graduated advances of salutation that well-bred men who are strangers to each other would use in Boston. . . . There is a grace and perfection . . . about these courtesies which could not be imitated by a Northern labourer where he designed to be extremely civil." In St. Augustine he "attended mass in the Catholic Church. The mass is in Latin and the sermon in English, and the audience, who are Spaniards, understand neither."

The dawning of the new year found him restless. He noted in his journal that "my best hopes [are] set aside, my projects all suspended. But," he went on, "the eye of the mind has at

CHAPTER 3

First Love

least grown richer in its hoard of observations." And in Florida he added to his roster of friends Achille Murat, nephew of Napoleon, and son of the King of Naples; with him he traveled back late in March to Charleston. He celebrated him in his journal under the date of April 6. "I have connected myself by friendship to a man who with as ardent a love of truth as that which animates me, with a mind surpassing mine in the variety of its research, and sharpened and strengthened to an energy for *action* to which I have no pretension, by advantages of birth and practical connexion with mankind beyond almost all men in the world,—is, yet, that which I had ever supposed only a creature of the imagination—a consistent Atheist,—and a disbeliever in the existence, and, of course, in the immortality of the soul. My faith in these points is strong and I trust, as I live, indestructible. Meanwhile I love and honour this intrepid doubter. His soul is noble, and his virtue, as the virtue of a Sadducee must always be, is sublime."

He paused in Alexandria, preached in Washington. He was now firm for the ministry, but still nourished dreams of becoming a poet, a scientist, a painter, or any kind of creative artist. In Philadelphia, visiting his schoolmate William Furness, now a Unitarian minister, he preached again. He ascended the pulpit again in New York, where William was practicing law, having turned his back on the ministry.

The Emerson family, meanwhile, was once again living with the Ripleys in Concord. Ralph joined them briefly, for the First Church in Boston had sent for him to preach; he was not offered a permanent pulpit, though he had some offers of a pulpit which he refused. In one of his new sermons he returned to his theme of compensation, declaring that "a system of Compensations prevails by God's will amid all the dealings of men in common life and that in virtue of this law, no man can enrich himself by doing wrong, or impoverish himself by doing right."

Soon he took a room in Divinity Hall. At Harvard he took his master's degree and took his exercise, as formerly, in walking, though at New Bedford, when he went to preach for Orville Dewey, a cousin, he took to sawing wood during the three weeks he remained there. Late in December, 1827, he left Divinity Hall to preach for three Sundays and on Christmas Day in Concord, New Hampshire. On that Christmas Day he met Ellen Louisa Tucker for the first time. It was a significant meeting, for it came at a time when he was complaining that he could not find the kind of friend he needed "either in the shape of man or woman." But there is nothing to show, in his writings, that he recognized in Ellen Tucker at this time that kind of friend.

He made an excellent impression in the pulpit at Concord, New Hampshire, but he returned to Cambridge, longing for better health so that he could accept the call to a pulpit somewhere in Boston. The year turned. Early in 1828 his brother Edward collapsed into mental illness, and presently his derangement deteriorated into violence to such a degree that he had to be placed in an asylum. Though he recovered, he remained permanently broken in health. Ralph thanked Providence that he need have no fear of insanity because he had been made with "so much mixture of *silliness*" in him that he was protected against it. He wrote of Edward in his journal: "My brother lived and acted with preternatural energy. My own manner is sluggish; my speech sometimes flippant, sometimes embarrassed and rugged; my actions . . . are of a passive kind. Edward had always great power of face. I have none. I laugh; I blush; I look ill-tempered; against my will and against my interest. But all this imperfection . . . is a defence."

With Charles now graduated from Harvard and studying law in Boston, Ralph found himself in charge of Edward's well-being. He savored a brief pleasure in being made an honorary member of Phi Beta Kappa in the summer of 1828, and listed himself in the Harvard catalogue for that year as a candidate for the regular ministry. In his journal he set down his firm belief that "The whole object of the universe to us is the formation of character."

He found time during the spring and summer of 1828 to visit in Concord, New Hampshire. He took occasion to renew his acquaintance with Ellen Louisa Tucker, who had clearly made more of an impression upon him than he had at first admitted to himself. The memory of her grew on him. One morning in June he wrote into her album a poem titled *Dreamings* that was clear enough as a declaration of love, for all its circumlocution.

> It was full pleasant—fraught with happiness,
> The dream that hath been over me! I would
> To Thee, dear Ellen, it were not all dross,
> The gold that makes my treasurings . . .
> . . . .
> . . . but the dream! and may I tell it to thee?
> To *thee,* who shap'd and who endued it
> With all its magical splendour and deep peace?

Perhaps he had Concord, New Hampshire, in mind as a pulpit. He needed some post in the country where he could care for Edward. He lost little time in accepting the invitation to come to Concord when it came. On December 6, 1828, he set out for that post with his brother Edward. He carried along a popular gift book which he listed in his account books as "for ELT."

For all his reticence, Ellen at least considered that he had been courting her in his own way for months. She was only seventeen, but was a dignified if frail young girl, oval of face, delicately featured, firm of purpose. She had determined to become his wife and saw no reason to lose any time. He had not been in Concord, New Hampshire, a month before, on December 24, he wrote his brother William, "I have the happiness to inform you that I have been now for one week engaged to Ellen Louisa Tucker a young lady who if you will trust my account is the fairest & best of her kind. . . . It is now just a year since I became acquainted with Ellen . . . but I thought I had got over my blushes & wishes when now I determined to go into that dangerous neighborhood again on Edward's account. But the presumptuous man was overthrown by the eye & ear & surrendered at discretion. He is now as happy as it is safe in life to be in the affection of the lady & the approbation of the friends. She is 17 years old, & very beautiful by universal consent. Her feelings are exceedingly delicate and noble—and I only want you to see her."

He was uncertain of his prospects; she did not wish to hear of them. She took pleasure in the love poems he inscribed in her album, and he added further verses to his own journal. He was so enamored of his affection for her that he undertook to preach in church on the subject of the affections. He either did not see or did not want to see an unfortunate tendency to physical weakness in Ellen's background—the early deaths of her father, a brother, and a sister, all of tuberculosis, the prevailing scourge of the times. Indeed, another sister was at that time lingering with that disease. Perhaps love blinded him to the threat that loomed over Ellen. Within a month of their engagement Ellen herself was ill with, as he wrote William, "that dangerous complaint   **27** which so often attackes the fairest in our stern climate. She has raised blood a week ago & I have been one of her nurses most unskilful but most interested. . . ."

Meanwhile, he had received a call to the Second Church of Boston, where Henry Ware was the pastor. He had preached for Ware; the congregation knew his ability at first hand. Ware had written late in December to prepare him for the invitation, and he had replied to express his gratitude but not without a demurrer: "I have affected generally a mode of illustration rather bolder than the usage of our preaching warrants, on the principle that our religion is nothing limited or partial, but of universal application, & is interested in all that interests man." He spoke also of some error to which Ware had made reference—perhaps he had been charged with not looking to the Scriptures with the same respect as other ministers did, which was a difference between them.

For a month he considered the invitation to become the junior pastor at Second Church. He was reluctant to leave Ellen's proximity, though her health had improved by January's end. Finally, on January 30, 1829, he replied to the Second Church and its governing society, accepting their invitation. "If my own feelings could have been consulted, I should have desired to postpone . . . for several months, my entrance into this solemn office. I do not now approach it with any sanguine confidence in my abilities, or in my prospects." His salary was to be $100 a month, but, should Ware resign—and his resignation could not long be put off, for Ware had given every intimation of it, not only to the congregation but also to Emerson—his salary would advance to $1800 a year.

On March 11, his ordination took place. Somewhat fore-
sightedly, Ezra Stiles Gannett, preaching on the occasion,

adjured the members of the society to respect their new pastor's independence of mind, of which Gannett, having been
graduated but a year before Emerson, had some first-hand
knowledge. Ralph's uncle Samuel Ripley preached the sermon
at the event, and grandfather Ezra Ripley gave the charge.
Emerson had the confidence of the majority of the members,
for there had been but five dissenting votes in the matter of
inviting him to the post of second pastor.

He gave himself as fully to his new obligations as his love
for Ellen permitted, for she was much of the time in Boston,
and he spent what time he could with her. He called on
the members of his congregation daily—averaging five such
visits each day—and he set about the preparation of sermons
though, as he wrote grandfather Ripley, "The prospect of
one each week, for an indefinite time to come is almost
terrifick." He prepared sermons on such subjects as the
ministry, conversation, the individual and the state, and religious liberalism.

Ellen's uncertain health troubled him. In June she was
taken ill again, "in the old way," he wrote his brother
Charles, "—very suddenly, & suffered in the night great distress, but the quantity of blood raised has not been much &
some symptoms her mother says are much less unfavorable
than at former times—but tis bad enough at the best & has
wonderfully changed my visit. I was perfectly happy now
I am watching & fearing & pitied."

Nevertheless, he maintained a firm separation between
his obligations to the society and the demands of his heart.
He set his course forthrightly in his first sermon after his
ordination and made no concession to Ware, however conscious of him in his audience he might be. He made his independence clear, even while paying tribute to Ware's virtues
as his senior colleague. It was plain that he expected to   *29*

exercise more freedom than some of the former pastors, that while he respected the Scriptures, it was his intention to speak more fully on right living than on the dogma.

Yet he was not satisfied, not happy, not easy in his position. He enjoyed sermons, but his congregation did not flock to hear him nearly as much as they came for some social affair. He disliked visiting the sick; he did not find it easy to make conversation, to comfort the ailing with platitudes from the Scriptures, and more than one of the sick complained of his awkwardness. He took what comfort he could in the reassurance of his friend Abel Adams, in whose house he lived, for Adams was somewhat more knowledgeable about human nature than about books, of which Emerson knew as much as anyone and more than most.

Ellen afforded him opportunities to desert his pulpit, to leave it to Ware despite the uncertainty of the senior pastor's health. Ellen, recovering from her recent illness, went off on a journey to the White Mountains. Emerson went along. He wrote his brother Charles that "we botanize & criticise & poetize & memorize & prize & grow wise we hope." He wrote Abel Adams, among others, to say how well Ellen bore the journeys they took—the first to the White Mountains, the second to the Merrimac River and into Connecticut— and to explain that, though he had been gone for much of that summer of 1829, he would soon be home and back at his preaching, for all that he had a lame leg.

His lameness did not prevent his marriage. He and Ellen were married on the last day of September, 1829, at the home of her stepfather, Colonel William Austin Kent, in Concord, New Hampshire. Early in October the young couple moved into the house of Mrs. Hannah Keating, not far from the Chardon Street home of his benefactor, Abel Adams. Emerson was now almost an invalid, for his

30

knee was inflamed. Yet he insisted upon preaching, after so long an absence, and did so while sitting.

Once his knee had improved, he threw himself into a program of self-improvement, subscribing to the Boston Athenaeum, buying books—by Montaigne, Cooper, Scott, Combe, Rousseau—and read others from the Harvard College Library, ranging from Marcus Aurelius and Plato to Southey and Goethe. He went on more journeys with Ellen, despite her occasional periods of "weakness." He added some obligations to his schedule in 1830, when he acted as chaplain of the state senate on election day in Boston, and was chosen to represent the fourth ward on the Boston School Committee, where he was assigned to the subcommittee on the Latin and Mayhew schools.

In the sermons that he wrote he returned to favorite themes with an unflagging persistence. In *Trust Thyself* he developed a little more of the doctrine of self-reliance within the framework of the sermon. "I wish to enforce the doctrine that a man should trust himself; should have a perfect confidence that there is no defect or inferiority in his nature; that when he discovers in himself different powers, or opinions, or manners, from others whom he loves and respects, he should not think himself in that degree inferior, but only different; and that for every defect there is some compensation provided in his system; and that wherever there is manifest imperfection in his character, it springs from his own neglect to cultivate some part of his mind. I am afraid of this great tendency to uniformity of action and conversation among men." He managed in one paragraph to touch upon his compensation doctrine and strike a blow against conformity, as he would do all his life.

The entries in his journal, still scant, included many a nugget. On November 5, 1830, he wrote: "When a man has got to a certain point in his career of truth he becomes conscious forevermore that he must take himself for better, for worse, as his portion; that what he can get out of his plot of ground by the sweat of his brow is his meat, and though the wide universe is full of good, not a particle can he add to himself but through his toil bestowed on this spot. It looks to him indeed a little spot, a poor barren possession, filled with thorns, and a lurking place for adders and apes and wolves. But cultivation will work wonders. It will enlarge to his eye as it is explored. That little nook will swell to a world of light and power and love."

He wrote less in his journal, and he wrote fewer letters. His duties as junior pastor at Second Church were sadly complicated by Ellen's uncertain health. He encouraged her writing of poetry, unwilling to acknowledge that she was not destined for success as a poet, but she was much given to sentimentality and wrote more from that spring than from the springs of inspiration.

As 1830 drew toward its close, her health continued to deteriorate. In January, 1831, Emerson contemplated setting out with her for Philadelphia and Baltimore "as soon as the snows melt . . . and as soon as she recovers her diminished strength so as to ride & walk," he wrote Edward Bliss Emerson, but added, "we have come to the prefixing of *if* to all our plans." All that month of January, Ellen was ill, despite days of seeming improvement. On the last day of the month he wrote William, "My poor Ellen has been sadly sick &, we flatter ourselves, is a little better. Nurse is rubbing her cold hands this moment to quicken her circulation."

Soon it was evident even to Emerson that Ellen was not long for this world. She lingered for another week, and at nine in the morning of February 8, 1831, died quietly. He had been resigned to it for some days, and two hours after her death wrote to his aunt Mary Moody Emerson, "My angel is gone to heaven this morning & I am alone in the world & strangely happy. Her lungs shall no more be torn nor her head scalded by her blood nor her whole life suffer from the warfare between the force & delicacy of her soul & the weakness of her frame. I said this morn & I do not know but it is true that I have never known a person in the world in whose separate existence as a soul I could so readily & fully believe & she is present with me now beaming joyfully upon me, in her deliverance & the entireness of her love for your poor nephew. I see it plainly that things & duties will look coarse & vulgar enough to me when I find the romance of her presence (& romance is a beggarly word) withdrawn from them all. But now the fulness of joy occasioned by things said by her in the last week & by this eternal deliverance is in my heart."

She was but nineteen and had been his wife less than a year and a half. He was never to be so moved by passion for anyone else as he had been moved by Ellen Tucker Emerson.

Whoso would be a man, must be a nonconformist. He who would gather immortal palms must not be hindered by the name of goodness, but must explore if it be goodness. Nothing is at last sacred but the integrity of your own mind. Absolve you to yourself, and you shall have the suffrage of the world. . . . No law can be sacred to me but that of my nature. Good and bad are but names very readily transferable to that or this; the only right is what is after my constitution; the only wrong what is against it. A man is to carry himself in the presence of all opposition as if every thing were titular and ephemeral but he. I am ashamed to think how easily we capitulate to badges and names, to large societies and dead institutions. Every decent and well-spoken individual affects and sways me more than is right. I ought to go upright and vital, and speak the rude truth always.

Self-Reliance

For a while after Ellen's death, he carried the wound of it. She had expressed a wish to be buried in her father's tomb in Roxbury, and now he walked daily to her tomb. Moreover, he wrote many poems to celebrate her and their life together. His mother's presence in their Chardon Street home did not alleviate the feeling of emptiness he felt. He held hard to his belief in immortality and took comfort in it, seeing Ellen in his mind's eye across the border. Indeed, his first sermon was on the subject of immortality.

His obligations at Second Church, however, left him less time than he would have liked in which to indulge his sorrow. After a dedicatory address on the occasion of the construction of a new vestry, he was obliged to deliver a course of sermons about the Scriptures, primarily for the young people of the congregation. He took little pleasure in the task, and found himself quibbling with his own conclusions, cankered by a first faint element of doubt, not so much of the Scriptures themselves as of the function of the minister in regard to them. Nevertheless, he persisted throughout that spring.

He had already written well over a hundred sermons and his views were on occasion somewhat unorthodox, if not sufficiently so to trouble anyone but the Reverend Henry

CHAPTER 4

Out of the Pulpit

Ware. Though he permitted nothing of this to escape him from the pulpit, he was beginning to question the divine authority of the New Testament, deliberately taking the unbeliever's view in order, he told himself, to strengthen his own faith.

He was also now serving his second year on the Boston School Committee, and was much troubled by difficulties at the Mayhew School, some teachers in which were the targets of much criticism. He was unmoved in his defense of the teachers and opposed a move to abolish corporal punishment in the public schools. He aroused enmities, and was not unhappy to be defeated for a third time on the committee.

Ellen was never far from his thoughts, and he was increasingly aware of his loneliness and isolation. "The days go by, griefs, and simpers, and sloth and disappointments," he wrote in his journal. "The dead do not return, and sometimes we are negligent of their image. Not of yours, Ellen. I know too well who is gone from me." And again: "I sit alone from month to month filled with a deep desire to exchange thoughts with a friend who does not appear."

To his brother Edward he wrote on April 20, 1831, "Her loss is a universal loss to me. It makes all life little worth & I go backward to her beautiful character for a charm that I might seek in vain thro the world. But faith is strong— her faith stronger than death & the scope of heaven is more distinct to me by the aid of affection such as hers." In August of that year, he summoned an old doctrine of his to sustain him, again in a letter to Edward: "That word *Compensations* is one of the watchwords of my spiritual world—& time & chance & sorrow & hope do not by their revelation abate my curiosity."

As his grief diminished slowly with time, his dissatisfaction with religion grew. More and more he stressed the individual. "The good man reveres himself," he wrote in a sermon on pride, "reveres his conscience, & would rather suffer any calamity than lower himself in his own esteem." He praised freedom of the will, and in his journal wrote, "The sermon which I write inquisitive of truth is good a year after, but that which is written because a sermon must be writ is musty the next day."

Early in 1832 he set down in his journal the objections that were taking strength in his mind. "It is the best part of the man, I sometimes think, that revolts most against his being a minister. His good revolts from official goodness. If he never spoke or acted but with the full consent of his understanding, if the whole man acted always, how powerful would be every act and every word. Well then, or ill then, how much power he sacrifices by conforming himself to say or do in other folks' time instead of in his own! The difficulty is that we do not make a world of our own, but fall into institutions already made, and have to accommodate ourselves to them to be useful at all, and this accommodation is, I say, a loss of so much integrity, and, of course, of so much power." He recognized, however, that a world of individualists might create insurmountable social problems. "But how shall the droning world get on if all its *beaux esprits* recalcitrate upon its approved forms and accepted institutions, and quit them all in order to be single minded? The double refiners would produce at the other end the double damned."

His discontent became evident, particularly to his brothers. His Aunt Mary thought he ought to remain in the ministry, in the tradition of his family. But he had not yet thought of leaving the ministry so much as of reforming the church. This problem was now uppermost in his mind; Ellen had receded; he could see her now, a year after her death, in perspective. Indeed, on March 29, 1832, he went to the tomb and, as he wrote laconically in his journal, "opened the coffin."

The conflict within him came in a disagreement about the method of administering the Lord's Supper. This was a public act the entire congregation could understand far better than any abstract idea of his own. He wrote the Second Church to advise his congregation about his changed view of the Lord's Supper and to suggest changes in administering it. The sacrament had been in dispute among some of Emerson's ancestors. The Second Church thought enough of him to appoint a committee to take his suggestions under advisement, but by summer, the committee's report, advising against any change in the method of administering the Lord's Supper, was accepted by the congregation, though the report was conciliatory toward Emerson.

He now faced a crisis of conscience. He was faced with the necessity of taking a step forward or one back. While the church building was closed for six weeks for repairs, he and his brother Charles set out on a journey to Conway, New Hampshire. There Charles turned back, and Emerson turned in upon himself, turning over and over in his mind the problem he faced. He saw that religion, to him, was "not credulity . . . not form." Religion, he now convinced himself, was something to be added to one's self. "It is to do right. It is to love, it is to serve, it is to think, it is to be humble." In his journal he put down, "I have sometimes thought that, in order to be a good minister, it was necessary to leave the ministry. The profession is antiquated."

What he meant to do was to bring the issue of the Lord's Supper to the entire congregation of Second Church in a sermon, and it was on this that he worked, making notes, writing paragraphs and lines. He climbed up Mt. Washington in a vigorous four and a quarter hours, as against the almost six it took most climbers. He had his sermon virtually ready for delivery when he returned home in July, but illness kept him from the pulpit.

Yet he had come closer to an irrevocable decision. On August 19, he wrote his Aunt Mary, "I have not yet come to any point with my people, my explanation being postponed by my ails, and have not come to any new point with myself. I remain of the same mind not prepared to eat or drink religiously, tho' it seem a small thing, & seeing no middle way, I apprehend a separation. This, tho' good nature & prudence condemn & possibly something else better than both, yet promises me much contentment & not the less opportunity of usefulness in the very partial & peculiar channel by which I must be useful if at all. The farthing candle was not made for nothing—the least leaf must ope & grow after the fashion of its *own* lobes & veins & not after that of the oak or the rose, and I can only do my work well by abjuring the opinions & customs of all others & adhering strictly to the divine plan a few dim inches of whose outline I faintly discern in my breast."

In September, at last—on the ninth—Emerson delivered his sermon on the Lord's Supper, a restrained, dignified statement of his decision, set forth with clarity and simplicity. He held that there was no valid authority for the administering of the Lord's Supper as it was being done. He said that though he respected those who disagreed with him, he would not go on observing the Lord's Supper in the manner approved by the Second Church, and by Christian sects in general.

Though he may have had some faint hope that the congregation might go along with him in his belief and relieve him of the obligation of observing the Lord's Supper, he did not really believe that he had carried the majority. Two days later, on September 11, he wrote a straightforward letter to the Proprietors of the Second Church of Boston requesting "a dismission from the pastoral charge." He added some few paragraphs designed to put his position more clearly. "I am very far from regarding my relation to you with indifference. I am bound to you, as a society, by the experience of uninterrupted kindness; by the feelings of respect & love I entertain for you all, as my tried friends; by ties of personal attachment to many individuals among you, which I account the happiness of my life . . .

"Nor do I think less of the office of a Christian minister. I am pained at the situation in which I find myself, that compels me to make a difference of opinion of no greater importance, the occasion of surrendering so many & so valuable functions as belong to that office." But he underscored again the resolution of his personal conflict. "I should be unfaithful to myself, if any change of circumstances could diminish my devotion to the cause of divine truth."

Whatever the future might hold, he had no intention at this time of making any break with his church or with the Christian faith. Before the month was out, he occupied the pulpit in Second Church again, and this time preached on self-reliance, his doctrine of which was taking stronger shape in his mind. In matters of religion he interpreted his doctrine to mean that the individual had no need of form or method to experience faith and to live in accordance with religious principles.

Despite his serenity and his firmness of purpose, his course was not an easy one. He poured his thoughts into his journal. As early as July 15, 1832, he had referred to his "hour of decision" and written: "It seems not worth while for them who charge others with exalting forms above the moon to fear forms themselves with extravagant dislike. . . . I know very well that it is a bad sign in a man to be too conscientious, and stick at gnats. . . . I cannot go habitually to an institution which they esteem holiest with indifference and dislike."

The pursuit of truth occupied many paragraphs in his journal. Truth was his goal. "The truth of truth consists in this, that it is self-evident, self-subsistent. . . . You don't get a candle to see the sun rise. Instead of making Christianity a vehicle of truth, you make truth only a horse for Christianity. It is a very operose way of making people good. . . . It does not shock us when ordinary persons discover no craving for truth. . . . but we cannot forgive it . . . that they who have souls to comprehend the magnificent secret should utterly neglect it and seek only huzzas and champagne."

The disciplines he knew were his own and much harsher than those the Second Church or any society might have imposed on him. He intended to be a leader of men, he meant to go about reaching his goals at the pace he set for himself, and the pulpit of any one church was clearly too narrow a base for him. He was concerned with more than forms and the philosophy of religion. He was concerned with something other than the freedoms he had as a preacher, with more than ceremonies and Christian rites. He was impatient with the failure of most of the people around him to see and understand the truths which to him were evident. For the same reason that he had no patience with teaching, he had none for the disciplines of the pulpit.

On October 28, 1832, the proprietors of the Second Church voted to accept his resignation, and to continue his salary until January. He set down the votes in his journal—thirty to   41 twenty, with four abstentions, not counting Abel Adams and others among his friends who had chosen not to attend the meeting.

He weathered the crisis. Not long after, he wrote laconically in his journal, "The chief mourner does not always attend the funeral." On November 19, he wrote his brother William, "the severing of our strained cord that bound me to the church is a mutual relief. It is sorrowful to me & to them in a measure for we were both suited & hoped to be mutually useful. But though it will occasion me perhaps some, (possibly, much) temporary embarrassment yet I walk firmly toward a peace & a freedom which I plainly see before me albeit afar."

He was now done with preaching at Second Church. He meant to occupy the pulpit once more to make a formal farewell, but ill health beset him, and instead, late that December, he sent a long letter which was read to the congregation from the pulpit and then later printed and distributed to the members.

He had plans for the future, but none firmly formulated in his mind. He thought of starting a new magazine in which he could set forth those truths he thought self-evident. He meant, in any case, to write, to hone the thoughts he had set down in his journal and shape them into more formal pieces for publication, perhaps, as well as for delivery from the lecture platform.

For the nonce, however, his health was his first concern. He was prevailed upon to go abroad. He sailed for Malta out of Boston on Christmas Day, in the brig *Jasper*, "236 tons, laden with logwood, mahogany, tobacco, sugar, coffee, beeswax, cheese, etc." He was but one of five passengers and endured a stormy passage and expressed his preference for "the latitude of 37°" over "my bitter native 42°." By February he was in Malta, filling himself with the sights and sounds of the Old World, but nevertheless aware that "wherever we go, whatever we do, self is the sole subject we study and learn."

He went from Malta to Naples and into Italy. He soon discovered that the Latin he knew was of little help to him and that his "knowledge of Italian & the ease of speaking it" had been overestimated. In Syracuse he broke off a bit of stone from the tomb of Timoleon and was impressed by the beggars of all ages who importuned travelers without end. He could not see everything, go everywhere he liked. "The fault of travellers," he wrote his brother William, "is like that of American farmers, both lay out too much ground & so slur, one the insight the other the cultivation of every part."

In Naples he found that "it is more than meat & drink to see so many princely old Greek heads Apollos, Dianas, Aristides, Demosthenes, Seneca and emperors & heroes without end." But the churches everywhere impressed him. "We, no doubt, shall continue in America, fancy free though we be, to build mean churches with pews for a thousand years to come," he observed in another letter to William. Despite all he saw, all the impressions crowding in upon him, he asked George Adams Sampson in a letter written in March, 1833, for "word of the Second Church. Tell me of it—particularly."

He reached Rome. There he visited the tomb of Tasso at the Church of St. Onofrio and saw the poet's bust. "Few things in Rome are better worth seeing than this head. What an air of independence & genius it hath!" he wrote Charles Emerson. He went to see Michelangelo's statues of Christ and Moses; he walked the corridors and galleries of the Vatican Museum; he was amused to be taken for "a priest in my own country" by a good Catholic hostess, who wondered whether his friends confessed to him, to which he replied, "All friendship is confession, is it not?" He saw Pope Gregory

XVI many times and was impressed anew with the grandeur and panoply of the Roman Catholic Church, however dubious he might be about some of its credos.

Of the first importance to him was not something he saw in Rome but something that came his way almost by accident. At a party at the home of his college schoolmate, Horace Gray, he met Gustave d'Eichthal, an acquaintance of Thomas Carlyle, whose own devotion to truth had long endeared his work to Emerson, and received from Eichthal a letter to John Stuart Mill in London, requesting Mill to introduce Emerson to Carlyle. Before leaving Rome, he wrote to his Aunt Mary, still troubled by his resignation from the ministry, to assure her that he was now mended in health, and to confess that he still sought "God's greatest gift"—a Teacher: "I know whilst I write thus that the creature is never to dawn upon me like a sun-burst I know too well how slowly we edge along sideways to everything good & brilliant in our lives & how casually & unobservedly we make all our most valued acquaintances. And yet," he believed now, "I saw Ellen at once in all her beauty & she never disappointed me except in her death."

He went on to Florence, where he dined with Walter Savage Landor, of whose *Imaginary Conversations* he had a very good opinion. He went to the Pergola and "it was a glorious show." He reflected in this beautiful city that "Perhaps the most satisfactory and most valuable impressions are those which come to each individual casually and in moments when he is not on the hunt for wonders." He wrote also in his journal during his stay in Florence: "No man can have society upon his own terms. If he seek it, he must serve it too. He immediately and inevitably contracts debts to it which he must pay, at a great expense, often, of inclination, and of time, and of duty."

From Florence to Venice and to Milan, the architecture of which seized upon his imagination, and caused his conclusion that architecture "seems to me ever an imitation." From Milan he journeyed to Paris, which pleased him less than he had expected it might. Perhaps, as he confided to his journal, "I have seen so much in five months that the magnificence of Paris will not take my eye." He left Paris to spend a few days in Geneva, where he saw Calvin's home. Back in Paris he listened to lectures at the Sorbonne, walked in the Jardin des Plantes, visited the Louvre and the Kings Library, went to the opera—"but whilst I see the advantages of Paris," he wrote to Samuel and Sarah Ripley, "they are not very great to me"—and paid a visit to Frascati's, the "most noted of the gambling houses . . . of Paris" where the "most perfect decorum and civility prevailed."

He reached London on July 20, on fire to achieve his primary goals in England—to meet Thomas Carlyle and Samuel Taylor Coleridge. He visited the British Museum which did not "appear so rich as one would expect from its fame," he wrote William, though "Its library is great." He was taken to see the home of Jeremy Bentham, the philosopher of utilitarianism, and to hear such preachers as Lant Carpenter, W. J. Fox, and Edward Irving. He witnessed the impressive funeral of Samuel Wilberforce, Bishop of Oxford.

At last he went to Highgate and called on Coleridge, who almost overwhelmed him with talk and readings from a manuscript, and monopolized such conversation as they had. Emerson thought him too old, too concerned with himself, to think with any new companion. If he had been somewhat disappointed in Landor, he was more so in Coleridge.

From Highgate he traveled to Scotland and the Lake Country, visiting Kenilworth and Warwick castles, Sheffield and York, and reached Edinburgh on August 16, where, on the following Sunday, he preached from the pulpit of the Unitarian Chapel on Young Street. Under the guidance of Alexander Ireland, he saw the city, and particularly places associated with Sir Walter Scott. Within a week he was on his way north to visit Burns's tomb and find Carlyle at Craigenputtock, in the parish of Dunscore.

With Carlyle, Emerson struck fire; the two men began a friendship that lasted throughout Carlyle's life. Carlyle, aware of his coming, made him stay the night. They talked and walked the wild country around. For all that Emerson thought Carlyle earthy and Carlyle thought Emerson an impractical visionary, the two men had so much in common, both of them seeking, each in his own way, to know what truth was, that the bond struck between them was an unbreakable one. Carlyle walked part of the way back to Dumfries with Emerson next day.

Emerson called it "a white day in my years," and wrote to Alexander Ireland of his enthusiasm. "He is a most simple frank amiable person—I became acquainted with him at once, we walked over several miles of hills & talked upon all the great questions that interest us most. The comfort of meeting a man of genius is that he speaks sincerely that he feels himself to be so rich that he is above the meanness of pretending to knowledge which he has not & Carlyle does not pretend to have solved the great problems but rather to be an observer of their solution as it goes forward in the world."

To his journal he admitted, "I found the youth I sought in Scotland, and good and wise and pleasant he seems to me. . . . Truth and peace and faith dwell with them (Carlyle and his pleasant wife) and beautify them. I never saw more amiableness than is in his countenance."

His next visit was to England's greatest living poet, William Wordsworth, at his home on Rydal Mount, near Ambleside.

He met a white-haired man wearing green goggles, but a poet "always young, and this old man took the same attitudes that he probably had at seventeen," he set down in his journal that evening, August 28, 1833. "His egotism was not at all displeasing, obtrusive, as I had heard. To be sure, it met no rock. I spoke as I felt, with great respect of his genius. . . . On my return to the inn, he walked over a mile with me, talking, and ever and anon stopping short to impress the word or the verse, and finally parted from me with great kindness and returned across the fields." To Alexander Ireland he wrote later of Wordsworth that he spoke against the evils of superficial education both in England and the United States, and thought "the intellectual tuition of society is going on out of all proportion faster than its moral training, which last is essential to all *education*."

He was now ready for home. In Liverpool on the first of September, he reviewed his tour of the Old World. "I thank the Great God who has led me through this European scene, this last schoolroom in which he has pleased to instruct me . . . and has now brought me to the shore and the ship that steers westward. He has shown me the men I wished to see,—Landor, Coleridge, Carlyle, Wordsworth; he has thereby comforted and confirmed me in my convictions. Many things I owe to the sight of these men. I shall judge more justly, less timidly, of wise men forevermore. To be sure, not one of these is a mind of the very first class, but what the intercourse with each of these suggests is true of intercourse with better men, that they never *fill the ear*—fill the mind—no, it is an *idealized* portrait which always we draw of them. Upon an intelligent man, wholly a stranger to their names, they would make in conversation no deep impression, none of a world-filling fame,—they would be remembered as sensible, well-read, earnest men, not more. Especially are they all defi-   47 cient . . . in different degrees . . . in insight into religious truth. They have no idea of that species of moral truth which I call the first philosophy. . . . But Carlyle is so amiable that I love him."

He set sail from Liverpool on the fourth of September. To his journal he confided at sea that he wished he "knew where and how I ought to live." He now had in mind a book about Nature. Contemplating religion and religionists, he concluded that "every form of Christian and of Pagan faith is . . . an imperfect version of the moral law." He was not yet utterly divorced from the pulpit, but well on the way to being so. "A man contains all that is needful to his government within himself. He is made a law unto himself. All real good or evil that can befall him must be from himself."

He landed at New York on October 7, 1833.

To go into solitude, a man needs to retire as much from his chamber as from society. I am not solitary whilst I read and write, though nobody is with me. But if a man would be alone, let him look at the stars. . . .

The stars awaken a certain reverence, because though always present, they are inaccessible; but all natural objects make a kindred impression, when the mind is open to their influence. Nature never wears a mean appearance. Neither does the wisest man extort her secret, and lose his curiosity by finding out all her perfection. Nature never became a toy to a wise spirit. The flowers, the animals, the mountains, reflected the wisdom of his best hour, as much as they had delighted the simplicity of his childhood.

Nature

Once home, he threw himself into preaching and lecturing. Early in November he addressed the Boston Society of Natural History on the advantages of studying natural history. Soon after, he went to New Bedford, Massachusetts, to preach. He wrote three lectures on natural history and studied geology, chemistry, and physics. He wrote Edward that he contemplated the publication of "a periodical paper which shall speak truth without fear or favor to all who desire to hear it." He was too busy to attend his brother William's marriage to Susan Woodward Haven in Portsmouth, New Hampshire, early in December, 1833, leaving Charles to represent the family at that event.

He could afford to take his leisure, if he so wanted, for he was finally being permitted, early in 1834, to draw upon his expected legacy from the estate of Ellen Tucker Emerson. But he was more often busy than not, with his writing, with lectures. He delivered *The Uses of Natural History: On the Relation of Man to the Globe,* and he began to write essays on representative men—Michelangelo, George Fox, John Milton, Martin Luther; these he read to his audiences.

He spent his time, when not on a tour, in Boston, or in Newton, Massachusetts, with his mother. In Newton he was closer to the woods and fields, and he took occasion to spend

CHAPTER 5

Second Marriage

days out of doors. On April 11, he went to Cambridge and spent most of that day at Mount Auburn—"got my luncheon at Fresh Pond, and went back again to the woods," he recorded that day in his journal. "And much wandering and seeing many things, four snakes gliding up and down a hollow for no purpose that I could see—not to eat, not for love, but only gliding; then a whole bed of *Hepatica triloba,* cousins of the Anemone, all blue and beautiful, but constrained by niggard nature to wear their last year's faded jacket of leaves; then a black-capped titmouse, who came upon a tree, and when I would know his name, sang *chick-a-dee-dee;* then a far-off tree full of clamorous birds, I know not what, but you might hear them half a mile; I forsook the tombs, and found a sunny hollow where the east wind would not blow, and lay down against the side of a tree to most happy beholdings. At least I opened my eyes and let what would pass through them into the soul. I saw no more my relation, how near and petty, to Cambridge or Boston; I heeded no more what minute or hour our Massachusetts clocks might indicate—I saw only the noble earth on which I was born, with the great Star which warms and enlightens it. I saw the clouds that hang their significant drapery over us. It was Day—that was all Heaven said. The pines glittered with their innumerable green needles in the light, and seemed to challenge me to read their riddle. The drab oak-leaves of the last year turned their little somersets and lay still again. And the wind bustled high overhead in the forest top. This gay and grand architecture, from the vault to the moss and lichen on which I lay,—who shall explain to me the laws of its proportions and adornments?"

On one such journey into the woods he turned again to verse, at which he had not been notably successful. But on this occasion, celebrating beauty for its own sake alone, he wrote one of his best poems in *The Rhodora: On Being Asked, Whence Is the Flower?*:

In May, when sea-winds pierced our solitudes,
I found the fresh Rhodora in the woods,
Spreading its leafless blooms in a damp nook,
To please the desert and the sluggish brook.
The purple petals, fallen in the pool,
Made the black water with their beauty gay;
Here might the red-bird come his plumes to cool,
And court the flower that cheapens his array.
Rhodora! if the sages ask thee why
This charm is wasted on the earth and sky,
Tell them, dear, that if eyes were made for seeing,
Then Beauty is its own excuse for being:
Why thou were there, O rival of the rose!
I never thought to ask, I never knew:
But in my simple ignorance, suppose
The self-same Power that brought me there brought you.

His long essay on Nature was much in his thoughts, but it suffered many interruptions. In July, 1834, he had the melancholy task of mounting the pulpit of Second Church for the last time to preach the funeral sermon of his good friend George Sampson. He gave such an effective sermon that he made a lasting impression not only on most of the audience, but also on Amos Bronson Alcott, a schoolmaster with pronounced liberal views, who had come to hear him speak, having some time before evinced a strong interest in Emerson. Sampson's death was a blow to him, but he was soon to withstand another; on October 1, 1834, his brother Edward Bliss Emerson died of tuberculosis in Puerto Rico. His loss, he wrote Thomas Carlyle later, "will be a lifelong sorrow." In   53 his melancholy, he wrote, Carlyle's letter—his first to Emerson in what was destined to be a long correspondence, replying to Emerson's first letter sent off in May—"made a bright light in a solitary & saddened place."

He sought the woods for contemplation. "No art can exceed the mellow beauty of one square rood of ground in the woods this afternoon," he wrote in his journal that autumn. "The noise of the locust, the bee, and the pine; the light, the insect forms, butterflies, cankerworms hanging, balloon-spiders swinging, devils-needles cruising, chirping grasshoppers; the tints and forms of the leaves and trees,—not a flower but its form seems a type, not a capsule but is an elegant seedbox,— then the myriad asters, polygalas, and golden-rods, and through the bush the far pines, and overhead the eternal sky. All the pleasing forms of art are imitations of these, and yet before the beauty of a right action all this beauty is cold and unaffecting."

In mid-October, Ruth Emerson and Ralph came to Concord to spend the winter with Ezra Ripley, though Emerson was off to preach in New York for several Sundays before he settled down in Concord, a place he loved above all others. He was now much surer of himself, of his purpose. "It is very easy in the world to live by the opinion of the world," he set down in his journal. "It is very easy in solitude to be self-centered. But the finished man is he who in the midst of the crowd keeps with perfect sweetness the independence of solitude." And he resolved: "Henceforth I design not to utter any speech, poem or book that is not entirely and peculiarly my own work. I will say at public lectures, and the like, those things which I have meditated for their own sake, and not for the first time with a view to that occasion."

During that year of 1834 he had another, more intimate concern. His fancy had been taken again by a young woman,

54

Miss Lydia Jackson. He had seen her first some years before, when, as a visitor in Boston, she had heard him preach at the Twelfth Congregational Church on Chambers Street. He had not met her on that occasion, but early in 1834 he had lectured in Plymouth, Massachusetts, where she lived. He visited in Plymouth subsequently and lectured there again. In January, 1835, he preached a midweek sermon in Plymouth and recorded in his journal, "Home again from Plymouth, with most agreeable recollections."

However much she was in his thoughts, he was as much in hers. Sometime in the course of that month he wrote her a proposal of marriage. She replied, asking him to come to Plymouth and talk the matter over. On the thirtieth of that month they were engaged. He was now in his thirty-second year, she almost a year older.

Two days later, he wrote her from Concord, "I delighted myself on Friday with my quite domesticated position & the good understanding that grew all the time, yet I went & came without one vehement word—or one passionate sign. . . . I merely surrendered myself to the hour & to the facts. . . . Yet am I well pleased that between us the most permanent ties should be the first formed & thereon should grow whatever others human nature will."

On February the fifth, he wrote his brother William to announce his engagement. "I announce this fact in a very different feeling from that with which I entered my first connexion. This is a very sober joy. This lady is a person of noble character whom to see is to respect. I find in her a quite unexpected community of sentiment & speculation, & in Plymouth she is dearly prized for her love & good works." He had clearly not been swept away by passion.

He left Lidian—as he preferred to call her ("my Lidian Queen")—in no doubt about a place for them to live. He needed "a sunset, a forest, a snow storm, a certain river-view" since these were "more" to him "than many friends & do ordinarily divide my day with my books. Wherever I go therefore I guard & study my rambling propensities with a care that is ridiculous to people, but to me is the care of my high calling." Concord, he wrote her without delay, was but one—he did not yet say the only one of such towns "in which I could find these necessary objects." But Plymouth did not seem to him such a town. "Plymouth is streets. I live in the wide champaign."

He pressed his claim for Concord as a place to live. In his next letter he said frankly, "For me to go to Plymouth would be to cripple me of some important resources & not so far as I see to do any work I cannot do here." He made clear, too, that his "empire" was divided between her and his "ink-stand," and that it would always be. He began house-hunting in Concord immediately, without the question being settled for her part, but in February he went to Plymouth to set his case for Concord more directly.

In March he was still singing Concord's praises. "Magical fitting of our eye to nature, that a few square miles of rocks bushes & water should present us under the changing light with such resplendent pictures & ever new transformations." By comparison, Plymouth was "but a seabeach." He defied her to say something for it. She must by this time have realized that in the matter of a place to live, at least, he was inflexible. Despite being as independent herself as her prospective husband and as much interested in the pursuit of truth as he, she did not after a while make any further claim for Plymouth. She came to Concord and met his family, who thought her not beautiful, but refined, unaffected, and a little peculiar—and so, no doubt, admirably suited to Emerson in their eyes.

In July Emerson finally found a house he could buy. It had been built by John Coolidge a few years previously and was situated just short of half a mile from the center of Concord. It occupied a trifle more than two acres, and extended from the street to the Mill Brook. It was an L-shaped house, with the kitchen and servants' quarters in the back, in the direction of the brook. He paid $3,500 for it and made a note of his purchase in his journal under the date of August 15.

Nevertheless, the impending wedding had to wait upon one more event, and that was the delivery on September 12 of an address of almost two hours' duration on the occasion of the second centennial of Concord, an address that was principally a history of Concord. But his preparation for it had involved many days of research—far more than he had ever undertaken for any previous lecture, for he was somewhat impatient with scholarly research, and his subjects did not in the main require it.

There was now no further reason for delay in his marriage. On the next day he set out for Plymouth in a chaise, paused the night in Boston, and in the late afternoon of September 14 reached his goal. They were married that evening, and early next morning began the return journey to Concord and the Emerson home on the Lexington Road.

Ruth Emerson having gone on a visit to New York, Lidian proceeded without delay to establish her own order. She added a second maid to the household, though she was somewhat taken aback when Emerson informed her that his financial resources were not limitless and that she must manage carefully. She was well satisfied with the order of their living, which began each day with prayers and ended it so. She wrote to her sister that Emerson was readily and willingly domesticated.

Indeed, he lent himself well to domestic life because the

routine exactly suited him, not because he was bent in that direction, for he was never bent in any direction against his will or inclination. So Lidian soon found, when the daily prayers were discontinued; she was more religious by training and inclination than he, despite the ready references he made to God and the divine meaning of things.

If anything, he was becoming less patient with organized religion. "Go into one of our cool churches," he wrote in his journal that autumn, "and begin to count the words that might be spared, and in most places the entire sermon will go. One sentence kept another in countenance, but not one by its own weight could have justified the saying of it." But he was not precipitate enough in his actions to make any break with the church; everything had to be thought through, and, insofar as the church was concerned, it took second place—as did all else—to his writing.

In this he continued to be very much his own man. His journal was filled with his beliefs. "A man to thrive in literature must trust himself. The voice of society sometimes, and the writings of great geniuses always, are so noble and prolific, that it seems justifiable to follow and imitate. But it is better to be an independent shoemaker than to be an actor and play a king." The theme of self-reliance, self-trust, self-belief, individuality occurred and recurred; scarcely a month went by without some reference, direct or indirect, to his favorite theme.

"A meek self-reliance I believe to be the law and constitution of good *writing*. A man is to treat the world like children who must hear and obey the spirit in which he speaks, but which is not his. If he thinks he is to sing to the tune of the times, is to be the decorus sayer of smooth things to lull the ear of society, and to speak of religion as the great traditional thing to be either mutely avoided or kept at a distance by civil bows, he may make a very good workman for the book-sellers, but he must lay aside all hope to wield or so much as to touch the bright thunderbolts of truth."

His articulate independence was now well known and widely advertised, but his status as a married man gave him enough of a conservative cast in the eyes of his Concord neighbors to warrant their electing him as a hog-reeve, which obligated him to assess fines against the owners of wandering pigs—though he very likely did not perform his duty, which was rather more traditional than active in 1836—and, shortly after, of electing him to a place on the school committee, of which he acted as chairman as well as serving as secretary. He was unhappy with both honors, and delegated as many of his duties as possible before he resigned.

He needed quiet and peace for contemplation and writing, though he did not cut himself off from Concord by any means. His brother Charles, now taking over Samuel Hoar's law office and contemplating marriage to his daughter, Elizabeth Hoar, came frequently to visit at the house, and was welcome at all times; his mother came from New York to make her home in the house; frequent visitors brought others—among them, Amos Bronson Alcott, to spend a weekend. "A wise man, simple, superior to display, and drops the best things as quietly as the least," judged Emerson.

He became a member of the Concord Social Library stand-ing committee. Now and then he preached in grandfather Ezra Ripley's church. On occasion he lectured for the local lyceum. His sermons notwithstanding—and the support he gave the church likewise—it was painfully evident to the more orthodox members of his family that Emerson was drifting away from religion and the church, and to none more so than Aunt Mary Moody Emerson who, however waspish she might be at the expense of person or tradition, looked the other way

59

when it came to matters of religion, and on one occasion so upset a dinner with her savage tongue that she brought about an estrangement with him, though not, she assured him, so much as to affect her "early admiration" of his genius.

Aunt Mary's estrangement did not trouble Emerson enough to disturb the tenor of his ways. He gave some time to the revision of a hopeless manuscript Alcott had thrust upon him, and wrote him at length about it, though all his paragraphs were not enough to conceal his impression that Alcott ought not yet to publish his work. The winter over, he engaged to lecture at the Salem Lyceum on English biography and literature, though, he wrote Lidian from Salem, he hated journeying. "The conversation of the stage coach I dislike also. On almost all occasions it is waste breath both what I hear & what I say. You will think me so nice & with so few things pleased that I am not fit to live. But I find my compensation in the heartiness of my joy when I do find my hour & my man. I have the morning of youth over again whenever I receive a thought or encounter an intelligent person."

His Salem lectures were interrupted by the need to take Charles to New York to be with his brother William, and their mother, who was currently visiting in that city. Charles's health had begun to fail him; a cough weakened him, and he was not able to travel to New York alone. He got as far as Boston, and there Emerson joined him and went with him to New York. Then he came back to Salem, waiting upon word of Charles's well-being, making plans for Charles to travel south at least for the month of May. "After 1 June, Massachusetts is a better climate," he assured William.

But plans for Charles's well-being were too late. His cough had but concealed a condition of advanced tuberculosis. In Boston Emerson received an urgent note from William and their mother to say that Charles had taken a turn for the worse. He wrote hastily to say that he and Elizabeth Hoar, Charles's fiancée, were setting out next day for New York. But on that May 9, the day of his letter to William, Emerson could not know that Charles had come in from a ride with his mother, fainted, and quickly died. He and Elizabeth Hoar arrived too late.

Emerson was deeply grieved. On the day after Charles's funeral he wrote to Lidian, "A soul is gone so costly & so rare that few persons were capable of knowing its price and I shall have my sorrow to myself for if I speak of him I shall be thought a fond exaggerator. He had the fourfold perfection of good sense, of genius, of grace, & of virtue, as I have never seen them combined. I determine to live in Concord, as you know, because he was there, and now that the immense promise of his maturity is destroyed, I feel not only unfastened there and adrift but a sort of shame at living at all."

He was no stranger to death, and he was possessed of more than an ordinary resilience. For all that, he wrote in his journal May 19: "Now commences a new and gloomy epoch of my life. . . . Who can ever supply his place to me? None. I may live long. I may . . . see many cultivated persons, but his elegance, his wit, his sense, his worship of principles, I shall not find united—I shall not find them separate. The eye is closed that was to see nature for me, and give me leave to see." Nevertheless, he continued his work without abatement.

He had, actually, no time to indulge his grief. There were letters to write, there were plans to form with Frederic Hedge a very special social circle to include Amos Bronson Alcott "with his Olympian dreams." ("He is a world-builder. Evermore he toils to solve the problem, whence is the world?") He entertained visitors, among them Margaret Fuller, a stu-   *61* dent of Goethe, who preached the same kind of intellectual freedom Emerson did; her visit stretched out to three weeks, and Emerson found her "a very intelligent person," a woman replete with ideas and voluble in their expression.

And he had to look forward to the publication of his first book, the proofs of which came to him "like a new coat, full of vexations" in the course of that summer. Early in September that first book was offered for sale in Boston—a slender volume of but ninety-five pages, entitled *Nature*.

*The man of talents who brings his poetry
and eloquence to market is like the hawk
which I have seen wheeling up to heaven
in the face of noon, and all to have a better
view of mice and moles and chickens.*
    The Journals of Ralph Waldo Emerson

Nature was the end product of many paragraphs in his journals and lectures, and of occasional thoughts projected in sermons and letters. It was Emerson's habit to review and rework his ideas until he achieved at least some temporary satisfaction with them. Having reached that plane with *Nature,* he permitted it to be published, though he did not attach his name to the title page. No reader at all familiar with Emerson's lectures could have any doubt about its author, however.

He proposed that man ought to "enjoy an original relation to the universe," one of individual insight rather than tradition. He defined the lover of nature as "he whose inward and outward senses are still truly adjusted to each other." Man is taught, he pointed out, "by great actions that the universe is the property of every individual in it," and "A life in harmony with Nature, the love of truth and of virtue, will purge the eyes to understand her text."

"A man's power to connect his thought with its proper symbol," he wrote, "and so to utter it, depends on the simplicity of his character, that is, upon his love of truth and his desire to communicate it without loss. The corruption of man is followed by the corruption of language. When simplicity of character and the sovereignty of ideas is broken up by the

CHAPTER 6

Nature and After

prevalence of secondary desires—the desire of riches, of pleasure, of power, and of praise—and duplicity and false-hood take place of simplicity and truth, the power over na-ture as an interpreter of the will is in a degree lost; new imagery ceases to be created, and old words are perverted to stand for things which are not; a paper currency is em-ployed, when there is no bullion in the vaults. In due time the fraud is manifest, and words lose all power to stimulate the understanding or the affections. Hundreds of writers may be found in every long-civilized nation who for a short time believe and make others believe that they see and utter truth, who do not of themselves clothe one thought in its natural garment, but who feed unconsciously on the lan-guage created by the primary writers of the country, those, namely, who hold primarily on nature."

"The moral influence of nature upon every individual is that amount of truth which it illustrates to him," he be-lieved, and "Each particle is a microcosm, and faithfully renders the likeness of the world." There was nothing of the conventional in *Nature,* and the philosophy it offered its readers was integral to Emerson. In his book, Emerson looked at nature from every perspective and achieved a kind of pan-theistic unity of man, God, and nature.

Nature was essentially a poet's book, rather than a philo-sopher's, an idealist's tract, rather than the fruit of profound experience. It was unconventional enough to attract attention and Emerson was moved by the notices it received to reflect on October 23, six weeks after its publication, that "The liter-ary man in this country has no critic," and on the twenty-ninth, "There is creative reading as well as creative writing."

On the whole, reaction to it was favorable enough, both critical and personal. It aroused some antagonism, but on the whole readers saw in it only what each of them wished to.

Even those critics who complained of the book's obscurity admitted that it was well grounded in eternal verities, and, since truth was always Emerson's ultimate goal, even he could not take offense at that.

Despite the fact that Emerson did not consider his book a brief for the Transcendentalists, this highly vocal group hailed it with delight. The Transcendentalists took their ideas from the laws of life and, like Emerson, were ever in search of truth, but in conscious experience and awareness, rather than in sense. They sought the ideal, and, again like Emerson, took a dim view of materialism. They held freedom of thought as the primary ideal, though they were not part of the Free-Thinker movement that took its origin in Europe. Perhaps the most energetic among them were Bronson Alcott, an idealistic pioneer in education, and the versatile and attractive Margaret Fuller.

Emerson was too much his own man to take any but a peripheral part in any formal organization. Not that the Transcendentalists could be called a formal or well-organized group, for, like most such groups, they were very largely too idealistic to lend themselves to so practical a thing as formal organization. But the social club he had been instrumental with Frederic Hedge in forming, which they had intended to call, after Plato, the Symposium, was soon known as the Transcendental Club. Its first meeting was held at the home of George Ripley less than a fortnight after the publication of *Nature*. Emerson was there, ever interested in new ideas, in intellectual conversation; so were Bronson Alcott, Hedge, Ripley, James Freeman Clarke, Orestes Brownson, and others, most of them in their thirties. A second meeting followed, this time at Alcott's home in Boston. The Transcendentalists attracted others of similar views, all truth-seekers, all impatient with creeds and traditions, and many of them min isters in the Unitarian church. Their outlook was liberal, and they were, most of them, confirmed idealists.

Emerson's association with the Transcendentalist movement was by no means all-engrossing, but rather more in the nature of an intellectual exercise of the kind in which he invariably took delight. He was not diverted from his own course in any way by his association with the Transcendentalists, and events at the Emerson home were untouched by Emerson's intellectual forays.

Late in October, Emerson's first child, a son to be named Waldo, was born. "Blessed child!" he wrote in his journal under date of October 31, "a lovely wonder to me, and which makes the universe look friendly to me." In a few days he went into the woods for "six hemlock trees to plant in my yard, which may grow whilst my boy is sleeping." The child fascinated him. "Every day a child presents a new aspect, Lidian says, as the face of the sky is different every hour, so that we never get tired. The truth seems to be that every child is infinitely beautiful. . . ."

He pushed on with his work, the preparation of a series of twelve lectures on the *Philosophy of History,* and had the first of them ready for delivery early in December. For this series, he chose to serve as his own business manager, having been previously disappointed in the management of his lectures; now he was willing to take the entire financial risk, and not share it or the proceeds with anyone else.

By early March he had completed the *Philosophy of History.* He estimated that his average audience consisted of three hundred-fifty people. He now entered upon an extensive period of lecturing, save for a brief period of uncertain health in the spring of 1837. His health improved—he thought in part because he worked more in his garden. Early in May, Waldo was baptized, "dressed in the self-same robe in which, twenty-seven years ago, my brother Charles was baptized."

He went often to the woods. He lived within easy walking distance of Walden Pond—to which he sometimes referred in his journal as "Walden Water"—and he was bent upon improving his acquaintance with nature. On May 9, 1837, he was delighted with a bee, which he "followed . . . with rhymes and fancies fine," ultimately turning to verse in *The Humble-Bee*:

> Burly, dozing humble-bee,
> Where thou art is clime for me.
> Let them sail for Porto Rique,
> Far-off heats through seas and seek;
> I will follow thee alone,
> Thou animated torrid-zone!
>
> Wiser far than human seer,
> Yellow-breeched philosopher!
> Seeing only what is fair,
> Sipping only what is sweet,
> Thou dost mock at fate and care,
> Leave the chaff, and take the wheat.
> When the fierce northwestern blast
> Cools sea and land so far and fast,
> Thou already slumberest deep;
> Woe and want thou canst outsleep;
> Want and woe, which torture us,
> Thy sleep makes ridiculous.

He kept his journal religiously. He observed on one occasion that "A man's wife has more power over him than the state has." He could hardly have been referring to his own domestic situation which revolved far more about him than about Lidian. Of Alcott, after a three-day visit at Emerson's home, he wrote, "He is, to be sure, monotonous. . . . one gets tired of the uniformity,—he will not be amused, he never cares for the pleasant side of things, but always truth and their origin he seeketh after." It was Alcott's deficiency in the sense of humor that troubled him, not his pressing search for truth, which was as genuine as Emerson's, if considerably more impractical.

He sang the virtues of gardening. "Yesterday afternoon, I stirred the earth about my shrubs and trees and quarrelled with the piper-grass, and now I have slept, and no longer am morose nor feel twitchings in the muscles of my face when a visitor is by." Ever and anon his childhood recurred to him. "I please myself with getting my nail-box set in the snuggest corner of the barn-chamber and well filled with nails, and gimlet, pincers, screwdriver and chisel. Herein I find an old joy of youth, of childhood, which perhaps all domestic children share,—the catlike love of garrets, barns and corn-chambers, and of the conveniences of long house-keeping."

But Emerson was not handy around the house and grounds. He was ill-equipped for repairs and alterations and all the many trivial obligations of keeping up a house and grounds, and what he did in this domain was principally a matter of casual inclination, not one of applied obligation. Whenever such work could be delegated to someone else, he avoided it.

He left Concord not only to lecture, but also for lyceum programs and public events. He went to Boston to see the Sac and Fox Indian delegation at the State House, "so savage in their head-dress and nakedness that it seemed as if the bears and catamounts had sent a deputation." He went to
Faneuil Hall to hear various politicians speak, under the

chairmanship of Daniel Webster. "The speaking was slovenly, small, and tiresome, but the crowd exciting, and the sound of the cheering extraordinarily fine." He mourned the murder of Elijah Lovejoy, the Illinois abolitionist who was lynched by a mob. "There are always men enough to die for the silliest punctilio . . . I sternly rejoice that one was found to die for humanity and the rights of free speech and opinion."

His reputation as a bold and forthright lecturer, not afraid of assailing the conventional and traditional, had grown. He received more invitations to speak than he cared to take. Late in August he was again asked to speak before the Salem Lyceum, by one I. F. Worcester, who added, according to Emerson's note in his journal under September 19, an odd stipulation: " 'The subject is, of course, discretionary with yourself, provided no allusions are made to religious controversy, or other exciting topics upon which the public mind is honestly divided!' I replied, on the same day . . . by quoting these words, and adding, 'I am really sorry that any person in Salem should think me capable of accepting an invitation so incumbered.' "

He had now embarked on a new course of lectures—entitled *Human Culture*—which he read at the Masonic Temple in Boston, and completed in ten lectures early in February, 1838. He noted in his journal that "the pecuniary advantage of the Course has been considerable," and set down as his net profit the sum of $568, at an average attendance of "about 439 persons" an evening. His journal also kept score of Waldo's learning to walk, of walks to Walden—once, to "read Goethe on the bank"—of public affairs, of the sale of his work— *Nature* had sold 500 copies in less than a month.

Nature brought him more disciples. Among them was a Concord neighbor, Henry Thoreau, who not only accepted Emerson's philosophy but gave it a flavor uniquely his own, and soon developed from it sterner disciplines than Emerson himself had envisioned. Thoreau struck Emerson's fancy. "I delight much in my young friend," he wrote early in 1838, "who seems to have as free and erect a mind as any I have ever met. . . . Everything that boy says makes merry with society, though nothing can be graver than his meaning."

The poet Jones Very—a discovery of his old friend Elizabeth Peabody's—came to call but thought Emerson too centered on himself and not enough of a mystic to suit him. Nevertheless, Emerson was sufficiently impressed with Very and his work to publish some of it the following year. Horace Mann, the educator, came and joined the circle at Coolidge Castle, as Emerson playfully called his home, now expanded to fill out its original L shape. His visitors included most of those men and women who called themselves Transcendentalists.

For all the comings and goings at the Emerson house, he remained essentially alone. However he may have welcomed disciples, he required of them nothing but that they think and bring forth challenging ideas. Religion continued to trouble him, and his journal gave evidence of it. "I regret," he wrote under the date of March 5, 1838, "that I did not state with distinctness and conspicuously the great error of modern society in respect to religion, and say, You can never come to any peace or power until you put your whole reliance in the moral constitution of man, and not at all in a historical Christianity.

"The Belief in Christianity that now prevails is the Unbelief of men. They will have Christ for a Lord and not for a Brother. Christ preaches the greatness of man, but we hear only the greatness of Christ."

Again, less than two weeks later: "There is no better subject for effective writing than the clergy. I ought to sit and think, and then write a discourse to the American Clergy, showing them the ugliness and unprofitableness of theology and the churches of this day, and the glory and sweetness of the moral nature out of whose pale they are almost wholly shut."

He sought his solitudes in nature, going as often as possible to Walden or along some country lane or into the woods. Yet he thought sometimes that solitude "is fearsome and heavy-hearted," admitting that he had "never known a man who had so much good accumulated upon him as I have. Reason, health, wife, child, friends, competence, reputation, the power to inspire, and the power to please; yet, leave me alone a few days, and I creep about as if in expectation of a calamity."

He walked out with Thoreau, exchanging ideas, sharing nature with him. "A crow's voice filled all the miles of air with sound." He walked with Alcott, who "looks with wise love at all real facts." He went occasionally to church, but was frequently tempted to go no more.

He steadily enlarged his reputation in everything he wrote, with every public appearance. His *Concord Hymn*, written for the dedication of the Concord monument commemorating the battle fought there on April 19, 1775, was delivered by grandfather Ripley in Emerson's absence on July 4, 1837; it was received with enthusiasm and gratification, from its first sonorous stanza:

> By the rude bridge that arched the flood,
>   Their flag to April's breeze unfurled,
> Here, once, the embattled farmers stood,
>   And fired the shot heard round the world.

to its last:

> Spirit, that made those heroes dare
>   To die, and leave their children free,

> Bid Time and Nature gently spare
> The shaft we raise to them and thee.

and was impressively sung on that occasion, after Ripley had read it, by the choir there assembled.

But his reputation grew as well on controversy, and two of his addresses aroused it. The first of them was the Phi Beta Kappa address delivered at Harvard in August, 1837, and later published as *The American Scholar*. His address lasted an hour and a quarter; in it Emerson called for an end to American dependence on "the learning of other lands," for the emergence of the man of culture, the thinking man, the self-reliant individual. He asked that "the single man plant himself indomitably on his instincts, and there abide," and wait upon "the huge world" to "come round to him." He declaimed the necessity for Americans to "walk on our own feet . . . work with our own hands . . . speak our own minds."

To Emerson's friends, who had heard him and read him, there was little new in what he said, but he had not said it so effectively before. It was, again, the theme of self-reliance—and through self-reliance, the fullest, most ideal realization of self.

His call to the scholar to live and act, not just to accept passively the ideas of men who had gone before—"Action . . . is essential. . . . Without it thought can never ripen into truth. . . . Only so much do I know, as I have lived"— aroused an instant response. He endured some criticism for his nationalistic call for American cultural independence, but the majority of his audience clearly understood that the primary theme was self-reliance.

The oration, printed, rapidly sold out, and the additional comment it stimulated added to Emerson's reputation. It was widely understood, too, among the listeners and readers of the oration that Emerson's plea for the involvement of the scholar in the active life of his time had reference to the social and intellectual problems of the age. In his journal he wrote of the "character in our abused age. The rights of woman, the antislavery-, temperance-, peace-, health-, and money-movements; female speakers, mobs and martyrs, the paradoxes, the antagonism of old and new, the anomalous church, the daring mysticism and the plain prose, the uneasy relation of domestics, the struggling toward better household arrangements,—all indicate life at the heart, not yet justly organized at the surface." Paradoxically, he himself tended to be cautious in his involvements.

The second and more controversial of his addresses was that delivered July 15, 1838, before the senior class of the Harvard Divinity School. He had been invited to deliver the address by the members of the class rather than by the faculty, and it was an admirable opportunity for him to crystallize his beliefs about the necessary reform of theology.

He began by praising the "perfection of this world in which our senses converse." He went on to the subject of the divine laws of which man is cognizant, and to the perfection of the supreme law. He soon reached the heart of his address—the need to reform the teaching of historical Christianity to the extent of eliminating such teaching altogether and seeing God without mediation. And the mediators —i.e., the ministers in the churches—were devoted only to formal religion. "Whenever the pulpit is usurped by a formalist," he cried, "then is the worshipper defrauded and disconsolate." He adjured the graduates "to go alone . . . cast behind you all conformity, and acquaint men at first hand with Deity. Look to it first and only, that fashion, custom, authority, pleasure, and money, are nothing to you—are not bandages over your eyes, that you cannot see—but live with the privilege of the immeasurable mind."

It was hardly to be expected that the clergy would hail

this address with delight. They were outraged. The faculty of the Harvard Divinity School were quick to dissociate themselves from the invitation that had been extended to Emerson. Conservative Boston leaders looked on Emerson as a radical bent upon upsetting the *status quo*.

The members of the Divinity School class who had invited Emerson to speak nevertheless printed 300 copies of the controversial address, setting off a flurry of related publications, led by the Unitarian Andrews Norton's *Discourse on the Latest Form of Infidelity*, a thinly disguised attack on Emerson and the Transcendentalists. Aunt Mary Moody Emerson, true to her cantankerous nature, sided with the attackers, not with her nephew.

Emerson was not much troubled by the attacks made upon him. To Henry Ware he wrote, "It strikes me very oddly & even a little ludicrously that the good & great men of Cambridge should think of raising me into an object of criticism. I have always been from my very incapacity of methodical writing a chartered libertine free to worship & free to rail lucky when I was understood but never esteemed near enough to the institutions & mind of society to deserve the notice of the masters of literature & religion." He observed in his journal, "As long as all that is said is said *against* me, I feel a certain sublime assurance of success, but as soon as honied words of praise are spoken for me, I feel as one that lies unprotected before his enemies."

A month later he wrote, "The taunts and cries of hatred and anger, the very epithets you bestow on me, are so familiar long ago in my reading that they sound to me ridiculously old and stale. The same thing has happened so many times over (that is, with the appearance of every original observer) that, if people were not very ignorant of literary history, they would be struck with the exact coincidence," confiding this to his journal among other comments, and promising that he had "a great deal more to say that will shock you out of all patience." Quite possibly he copied the passage from a letter to one of his correspondents, for the controversy over the Divinity School address had increased the flow of mail to Coolidge Castle, and Emerson was hard put to it to answer all the letters he received, both of criticism and praise, particularly since, as he had written Margaret Fuller earlier that year, "I seldom write one [a letter] unless my belief in immortality is at the moment very strong and so indulges me in a free use of time."

Two months after he had delivered the controversial address, and the storm had subsided a little, he wrote laconically in his journal, "What is the hardest task in the world? To think . . ." In his journal, too, he cautioned himself not to fall into the error of "dreaming that I am persecuted whenever I am contradicted. No man, I think, had ever a greater well-being with a less desert than I. I can very well afford to be accounted bad or foolish by a few dozen or a few hundred persons,—I who see myself greeted by the good expectation of so many friends far beyond any power of thought or communication of thought residing in me. Besides, I own, I am often inclined to take part with those who say I am bad or foolish, for I fear I am both."

Though the controversy about the Divinity School address died down, there remained a simmering resentment, particularly among the Unitarian and Congregational clergy. It accomplished for Emerson what he had not been able to bring himself to before this—it ended his career as a preacher. Though he preached in Watertown, and in Concord, his last appearance in the pulpit as a preacher was on January 20, 1839, in his grandfather Ripley's church.

*To believe your own thought, to believe that
what is true for you in your private heart,
is true for all men,—that is genius. Speak
your latent conviction, and it shall be the
universal sense; for always the inmost in
due time becomes the outmost,—and our
first thought is rendered back to us by the
trumpets of the Last Judgment. . . . A man
should learn to detect and watch that gleam
of light which flashes across his mind from
within, more than the lustre of the
firmament of bards and sages.*

Self-Reliance

Emerson was now approaching the zenith of his power, the peak of his reputation. He opened 1839 with a course of lectures entitled *Human Life* in Boston. In February he hailed the birth of his daughter Ellen, on the twenty-fourth, "a soft, quiet, swarthy little creature, apparently perfect and healthy." It was Lidian, who, having learned from him all about his first wife, named his "little winter bud."

As the spring of that year ran out, he exulted in his journal that his life was "a May game, I will live as I like. I defy your strait-laced, weary social ways and modes. Blue is the sky; green the fields and groves, fresh the springs, glad the rivers, and hospitable the splendor of sun and star. I will play my game out."

Visitors continued to come to Coolidge Castle, none more frequently than Alcott, of whom he wrote to Margaret Fuller that no one had yet done justice to "his towering genius." Jones Very came to stay two or three days, "serene, intelligent & true in all the conversation I have had with him," though Very was disturbed. Emerson was soon at the editing of Very's book of poems, and reading poems brought to him in manuscript by Thoreau, of whose poem *Sympathy* he wrote

CHAPTER 7

The Essays

in his journal, "The purest strain, and the loftiest, I think, that has yet pealed from this unpoetic American forest."

He worked his garden, smoothing his "temper," as he put it, drawing out his own "splinters," and he walked through the fields and woods that surrounded Concord. "When I walk in Walden wood," he wrote in July, "I seem to myself an inexhaustible poet, if only I could once break through the fence of silence, and vent myself in adequate rhyme." But his own poetry was reluctant to come. "I should tell you," he wrote Margaret Fuller, later that summer, "how much I pine to write verses, & cannot. The wind, the water, the ferns do all but coin themselves into rhymes before me, yet the last step of the alchemy fails." He was still in no mood for poetry in September, when he made a journey into New Hampshire through the Franconia Notch, although the Sphinx struck him as "a fine subject for verse."

In midmonth the members of the Transcendental Club, Emerson among them, decided to bring out a magazine in which the Transcendentalists and their friends could publish their papers and their verse. Emerson evaded the editing of it in favor of Margaret Fuller, but he worked in its behalf. The magazine, he wrote his brother William, was "for the exposition of absolute truth," though he was dubious about its coming into being; he would contribute to it, and so, he thought, would "my Henry Thoreau." He suggested contributors for it, in addition to Thoreau—Caroline Sturgis, Sarah Freeman Clarke, young Ellery Channing, Samuel Gray Ward, and others. He wrote most of the introductory essay for the initial issue. The journal was titled *The Dial,* and its first issue appeared in July, 1840. It proved to be more literary than anything else, and he deplored the absence of economic and political matter.

The affairs of *The Dial* did not much interrupt his work—

not nearly so much as visitors. Though he delighted in visitors, and frequently prevailed upon them to stay longer than they had intended, he admitted in his journal that "What is good to make me happy is not however good to make me write. Life too near paralyses art." He deplored, too, his lack of system: "I need hardly say to anyone acquainted with my thoughts that I have no System. When I was quite young, I fancied that by keeping a manuscript Journal by me . . . I should be able to complete a sort of encyclopaedia containing the net value of all the definitions at which the world had yet arrived."

Nevertheless, he managed to put together a new course of ten lectures under the title of *The Present Age,* and delivered them on ten consecutive Wednesday evenings in the course of that winter in Boston, closing the series on the twelfth of February, 1840. But "these lectures give me little pleasure," he wrote in his journal. The journal, however, he kept faithfully, recording his thoughts, impressions, celebrating nature and his friends; he would not, he recorded, like the rich "live for show"; he set down that "I, who suffer from excess of sympathy, proclaim always the merits of self-reliance"; he reflected that "An apple-tree near at hand is a great awkward flower, but seen at some distance it gives a wonderful softness to the landscape."

He deplored the materialism of his age. "In New York, in Boston, in Providence, you cannot pass two men in the street without the word escaping them in the very moment of encounter, 'dollars,' 'two and a half per cent,' 'three per cent.'" Bronson Alcott was sometimes too much with him and became "a tedious archangel," but Thoreau held his own in his affections: "The good river-god has taken the form of my valiant Henry Thoreau here and introduced me to the riches of his shadowy, starlit, moonlit stream, a lovely new world lying as close and yet as unknown to this vulgar trite one of streets and shops as death to life, or poetry to prose."

But his primary creative work was in the preparation of his first volume of essays for publication. He had dreamed since youth of publishing such a book, and now at last he was shaping the first collection for the printer. On the first of January, 1841, he sent his "little book" to the printer; in March it appeared, titled simply *Essays,* though Emerson had first thought of calling it *Forest Essays.* Very soon after, it appeared also in England, sponsored there by Carlyle, whose work Emerson had busily forwarded in America ever since he had met Carlyle, and with whom he continued to correspond.

The essays in his second book were the product of many journal notes, lectures, and other writings. He chose to write about twelve subjects, from history—which he now thought a better key to the divine law than nature—to art, but the subjects to which he did the most adequate justice were those about which he had thought and written for many years— self-reliance, compensation, love, friendship. The essays, titled after their subjects, were filled with nuggets that were readily stored in the minds of his readers.

Self-Reliance particularly rang with lines and paragraphs, honed and refined into final statements, long familiar to Emerson's readers. "There is a time in every man's education when he arrives at the conviction that envy is ignorance; that imitation is suicide; that he must take himself for better for worse as his portion; that though the wide universe is full of good, no kernel of nourishing corn can come to him but through his toil bestowed on that plot of ground which is given to him to till. The power which resides in him is new in nature, and none but he knows what that is which he can do, nor does he know until he has tried. . . . Society everywhere is in conspiracy against the manhood of every one of its members."

He struck hard at conformity. "Whoso would be a man, must be a nonconformist. . . . I do not wish to expiate, but to live. My life is for itself and not for spectacle. I much prefer that it should be of a lower strain, so it be genuine and equal, than that it should be glittering and unsteady. . . . What I must do is all that concerns me, not what the people think. This rule, equally arduous in actual and in intellectual life, may serve for the whole distinction between greatness and meanness. It is the harder because you will always find those who think they know what is your duty better than you know it. It is easy in the world to live after the world's opinion. . . . The objection to conforming to usages that have become dead to you is that it scatters your force. . . . But do your thing, and I shall know you. . . . A foolish consistency is the hobgoblin of little minds. . . . Speak what you think now in hard words, and tomorrow speak what tomorrow thinks in hard words again, though it contradict everything you said today."

Memorable lines were dropped like jewels throughout *Self-Reliance,* destined to be quoted, reprinted, and heard here and abroad. "To be great is to be misunderstood. . . . We pass for what we are. Character teaches above our wills. . . . The force of character is cumulative. . . . Let a man then know his worth, and keep things under his feet. . . . An institution is the lengthened shadow of one man. . . . Travelling is a fool's paradise. . . . Insist on yourself; never imitate. . . . Society acquires new arts and loses old instincts. . . . The civilized man has built a coach, but has lost the use of his feet. . . . A political victory, a rise of rents, the recovery of your sick or the return of your absent friend, or some other favorable event raises your spirits, and you think good days are preparing for you. Do not believe it. Nothing can bring you peace but yourself. Nothing can bring you peace but the triumph of principles."

Self-Reliance was a compendium of all the wisdom on the subject he had gathered over the years. There were reflections of Montaigne, folk wisdom, Hindu philosophy; these were woven together with Emerson's own conclusions, and the whole essay was in effect a statement of basic Transcendental philosophy. But it was only incidentally so—it was actually the cornerstone of Emerson's own philosophy. The essay had equal parts of intuition, mysticism, and idealism and made a wide appeal to the kind of individualism that flourished particularly in New England and was to be found in its most primitive form all along the Western frontier.

Compensation rose from Emerson's personal concern with the tragedies he had suffered—the deaths of Ellen, of Edward and Charles particularly, as well as his own periods of uncertain health. It was also a refutation of the doctrine put forth in the churches, that "judgement is not executed in this world; that the wicked are successful; that the good are miserable." Next to self-reliance, compensation was the subject that had been most frequently mentioned in the early journals; it had occupied Emerson for many years.

This essay, too, was filled with quotations refined from his journals. "Men are better than their theology. . . . For everything you have missed, you have gained something else; and for everything you gain, you lose something. . . . the universe is represented in every one of its particles. . . . The world globes itself in a drop of dew. . . . All things are double, one against another. . . . A wise man will . . . know that it is the part of prudence to face every claimant and pay every just demand on your time, your talents, or your heart. Always pay; for first or last you must pay your entire debt. . . . the real price of labor is knowledge and virtue, whereof wealth and credit are signs. . . . The absolute balance of Give and Take, the doctrine that everything has its price—and if that

84

price is not paid, not that thing but something else is obtained, and that it is impossible to get anything without its
price—is not less sublime in the columns of a ledger than in
the budgets of states, in the laws of light and darkness, in all
the action and reaction of nature. . . . As no man thoroughly
understands a truth until he has contended against it, so no
man has a thorough acquaintance with the hindrances or
talents of men until he has suffered from the one and seen the
triumph of the other over his own want of the same."

Some lines came unaltered from his journal, from earlier
lectures. "It is as impossible for a man to be cheated by anyone but himself, as for a thing to be and not to be at the same
time. . . . Everything has two sides, a good and an evil. . . .
There is a deeper fact in the soul than compensation, to wit,
his own nature. . . . There can be no excess to love, none to
knowledge, none to beauty, when these attributes are considered in the purest sense. . . . Man's life is a progress, and
not a station. His instinct is trust."

Some reflections on his own tragedies closed *Compensation,* but in *Spiritual Laws,* the essay that followed it in his
collection, he returned to the theme. "All loss, all pain, is particular; the universe remains to the heart unhurt." And again:
"The soul will not know either deformity or pain. . . . it is
only the finite that has wrought and suffered; the infinite lies
stretched in smiling repose."

In *Love* Emerson celebrated spiritual rather than physical
love; he saw the course of love to the spiritual plane from
the physical experience. His essay embodied much of Plato,
especially the *Phaedrus* and the *Symposium,* but only such
parts as Emerson could accept within his own experience.
"Little think the youth and maiden who are glancing at each
other across crowded rooms with eyes so full of mutual intelligence, of the precious fruit long hereafter to proceed from

this new, quite external stimulus. The work of vegetation begins first in the irritability of the bark and leaf-buds." Clearly, he held, "we are put in training for a love which knows not sex, nor person, nor partiality, but which seeks virtue and wisdom everywhere, to the end of increasing virtue and wisdom."

Friendship, on the other hand, had a wider basis in his personal experience than did *Love,* for Emerson's passion was principally for ideas. "Friendship, like the immortality of the soul, is too good to be believed. . . . every man passes his life in the search after friendship." How many times he had set down in his journal his longing for that one friend in whom he could confide every thought, with whom he could discuss all things! "Our friendships hurry to short and poor conclusions, because we have made them a texture of wine and dreams, instead of the tough fibre of the human heart." He stressed the element of tenderness in friendship, but the more important element was, plainly, truth. With a friend he saw himself as "arrived at last in the presence of a man so real and equal that I may drop even those undermost garments of dissimulation, courtesy, and second thought, which men never put off, and may deal with him with the simplicity and wholeness with which one chemical atom meets another. Sincerity is the luxury allowed, like diadems and authority, only to the highest rank; *that* being permitted to speak truth, as having none above it to court or conform unto. . . .

"Friendship may be said to require natures so rare and costly, each so well tempered and so happily adapted, and withal so circumstanced . . . that its satisfaction can very seldom be assured. . . . Friendship requires that rare mean betwixt likeness and unlikeness that piques each with the presence of power and of consent in the other party. . . . Better be a nettle in the side of your friend than his echo. . . . The only reward of virtue is virtue; the only way to have a friend is to be one. . . . The essence of friendship," he concluded, "is entireness, a total magnanimity and trust."

The theme of self-reliance was threaded through some of the essays apart from that bearing the title, particularly *Heroism* and *The Over-soul,* and the theme of truth informed most of the essays. The book, taken in part or whole, was the essence of Emerson's philosophy; it praised his independence of thought, for all that his wide reading had contributed to the writing of many of the essays. He had distilled the knowledge he had gleaned from his reading, filtered it through his awareness, measured it against his experience.

The book met with a mixed reception. Emerson's followers hailed it with pleasure, but those who had had some doubts about his orthodoxy or his faith or even his common sense were confirmed in their doubts by the essays. His aunt Mary Moody Emerson called the book a mixture of atheism and false independence and harked back to the boy he had been, "so mild, candid, modest, obliging." She thought the book an offense against Christianity; she thought it disgraced her nephew. Some reviewers quarrelled with Emerson's doctrine of self-reliance, fearing for the *status quo.* Edward Everett thought the book nonsense, though Carlyle endorsed it, however much he felt that Emerson had not been quite successful in catching the universe in his net.

Moreover, it did not earn Emerson much in the way of financial reward—but none of his writings brought in nearly as much income as his securities did. He had invested much of his legacy from Ellen Tucker Emerson, and his investments made the sound basis of his income. His lectures earned more than his books, and he found it necessary in the summer and autumn to prepare yet another series of eight lectures entitled *On the Times.*

If he felt any concern over the reception of his *Essays,* he revealed none of it. One observation in his journal under the date of June 7, 1841, reflected his views on critics. "The borer on our peach trees bores that she may deposit an egg: but the borer into theories and institutions and books bores that he may bore." He took a holiday at Nantasket Beach, "This vastness & roar—the rubbing of the sea on the land so ancient & pleasant a sound, the color & the curve of the same do fill & content the eye as mountains & woods do not," he reported to Lidian.

That summer, for the second time, Mary Russell spent with the Emerson children as governess. That summer, too, Henry Thoreau came to stay at the Emerson house: "a scholar & a poet & as full of buds of promise as a young apple tree," Emerson wrote his brother William. "He is to have his board & for what labor he chooses to do: and he is thus far a great benefactor & physician to me for he is an indefatigable & a very skilful laborer & I work with him as I should not be without him. . . ."

But Thoreau was prickly; Emerson was the more flexible of the two, for he was forever refining and reshaping his thoughts, effecting changes, while Thoreau tended rather more to polish and restate without fundamental change. Emerson, too, had the impression that Thoreau was in every sense his disciple, which was not true. "I told Henry Thoreau that his freedom is in the form, but he does not disclose new matter," he set down in his journal. "I am very familiar with all his thoughts,—they are my own quite originally drest. But if the question be, what new ideas has he thrown into circulation, he has not yet told what that is which he was created to say. I said to him what I often feel, I only knew three persons who seem to me fully to see this law of reciprocity or compensation,—himself, Alcott, and myself: and 't is odd that we should all be neighbors, for in the wide land or the wide earth I do not know another who seems to have it as deeply and originally as these three Gothamites."

On the threshold of autumn that year Dr. Ezra Ripley died at the age of ninety. "The fall of this oak of ninety years makes some sensation in the forest, old and doomed as it was," he noted in his journal. To his brother William he added that the old man's face "has the roundness & the resolution of manhood. He has been a very temperate man. You may judge we feel as if the patriarch of the tribe was fallen in this just, kind, & companionable old man, whose character was so thoroughly intelligible that every child could read him." This grandfather of his had, no matter how distressed he might have been at Emerson's cleavage from the Scriptural lessons, steadfastly refused to condemn him.

On occasion Emerson visited Brook Farm, the Transcendental experimental community at West Roxbury, though he had resolutely refused to associate himself formally with it. Sometimes he attended their picnics, though it was not quite true even as an oversimplification that Brook Farm was, as he later described it, "a perpetual picnic." He was interested in the community principally as an observer. Moreover, many of his friends belonged to it, and he could always be assured of stimulating conversation, and a remarkable proliferation of ideas of the kind he enjoyed exploring. He was not, however, convinced that Brook Farm would succeed in its object and convince the world that such communal living was indeed the direction which society must take. He was, furthermore, no friend of organized reform; he believed that only a reform of human nature, something more basic than organized reform, would effect change enough to eliminate class distinctions and alleviate the plight of the workers.

Two months after Dr. Ripley's death, another daughter was

born at Coolidge Castle. The little girl was named Edith. She seemed to her father "to be more than a thousand years old. She came into the house naked and helpless, but she had for her defence more than the strength of millions."

His joy in the birth of his second daughter was soon blighted by another tragedy, the most agonizing of his life. Late in January his son Waldo took sick with scarlet fever and in four days was dead. Ellen survived the fever. For five years Waldo had been Emerson's delight; his death left Emerson grief-stricken. He poured his sorrow into a spate of letters and entered it in his journal.

On the morning after the boy's death he recorded that he woke at three o'clock to the crowing of cocks in the barnyards. "The sun went up the morning sky with all his light, but the landscape was dishonored by this loss. For this boy, in whose remembrance I have both slept and waked so oft, decorated for me the morning star, the evening cloud, how much more all the particulars of daily economy; for he had touched with his lively curiosity every trivial fact and circumstance in the household.

"A boy of early wisdom, of a grave and even majestic deportment, of a perfect gentleness.

"Every tramper that ever tramped is abroad, but the little feet are still.

"He gave up his little innocent breath like a bird."

In a few days he added, "Sorrow make us all children again,—destroys all differences of intellect. The wisest knows nothing."

A week later he could write to Margaret Fuller that "we are finding again our hands & feet after our dull & dreadful dream which does not leave us where it found us," but as late as March 20, he referred to Waldo's death in his journal

when he wrote, "I comprehend nothing of this fact but its

bitterness. Explanation I have none, consolation none that rises out of the fact itself; only diversion; only oblivion of this, and pursuit of new objects."

The boy's death shook not only Emerson's philosophy but also Lidian's. She turned back from Transcendentalism to a more orthodox religion. He had nowhere to turn. He had never been Unitarian or Transcendentalist so much as he had been Emersonian, but his resignation to Waldo's death found expression at last in the long *Threnody* he wrote in his memory:

> The South-wind brings
> Life, sunshine and desire,
> And on every mount and meadow
> Breathes aromatic fire;
> But over the dead he has no power,
> The lost, the lost, he cannot restore;
> And, looking over the hills, I mourn
> The darling who shall not return . . . .

There is no power of expansion in men. Our friends early appear to us representatives of certain ideas which they never pass or exceed. They stand on the brink of the ocean of thought and power, but they never take the single step that would bring them there. A man is like a bit of Labrador spar, which has no lustre as you turn it in your hand until you come to a particular angle; then it shows deep and beautiful colors. There is no adaptation or universal applicability in men, but each has his special talent, and the mastery of successful men consists in adroitly keeping themselves where and when that turn shall be oftenest to be practised. We do what we must, and call it by the best names we can . . .

Experience

Emerson now threw himself into as many activities as he could, to help take his thoughts away from his dead son, to resume the even tenor of his existence. Before that winter of 1842 was done, he lectured in Providence and New York. In New York he read six of his lectures in the series *On The Times* and earned $200, "after all expenses were paid." He widened his circle of acquaintances in the city, meeting, among others, Horace Greeley, Albert Brisbane, and Henry James, visiting again with William Cullen Bryant, whose poetry was far more widely read than his own. His lectures, he noted in his journal, "had about the same reception there as elsewhere: very fine and poetical, but a little puzzling. One thought it 'as good as a kaleidoscope.' Another, a good Staten Islander, would go to hear, 'for he had heard I was a rattler.' "

His new acquaintances impressed him. He wrote Margaret Fuller that Greeley was "a young man with white soft hair from New Hampshire . . . of sanguine temper & liberal mind, no scholar but such a one as journals & newspapers make, who listens after all new thoughts & things but with the indispensable New York condition that they can be made available. . . ." As for Brisbane, "the socialist," who believed

CHAPTER 8

The Second Book of Essays

that François Marie Fourier, his fellow socialist who wished to reorganize society into phalanxes, had "completely established" the "immorality of the soul"—he was eager to convert Emerson to Fourierism. But the city left him cold; "the expression of the faces of the male & female crowd in Broadway, the endless rustle of newspapers all make me feel not the value of their classes, but of my own class—the supreme need of the few worshippers of the Muse—wild & sacred—as counteraction to this world of material & ephemeral interest."

He was glad to be home again. He breathed more easily in Concord where he knew that continuity of time and place so necessary to him. There Alcott, who was bound for England, applied to him for a letter of introduction to Carlyle; Emerson asked himself what he must say of him whom he saw as "a man of ideas, a man of faith. Expect contempt for all usages which are simply such. His social nature and his taste for beauty and magnificence will betray him into tolerance and indulgence, even, to men and to magnificence, but a statute or a practice he is condemned to measure by its essential wisdom or folly." He set this down in his journal but wrote to Carlyle that he ought not to let Alcott "go quite out of reach" until he could be sure he had "seen him & know for certain the nature of the man."

In March his correspondence with Margaret Fuller took an unexpected turn when she let it be known that she intended to abandon her editing of *The Dial*. He was disturbed. "That you should be such a lavish spender of time labor & health for our poor Dial, with such a bankrupt's return, makes me very sorry." Nevertheless, he was unwilling to see the magazine die. He thought perhaps that Theodore Parker might be approached to edit it, as she had suggested. She had also suggested Emerson, but it was characteristic of him that he should think first of Parker, rather than himself. Parker, a preacher and social reformer, was a proponent of a more rationalistic theology, much denounced by his fellow clergymen. He had been interested in Transcendentalism and had taken part in the activities at Brook Farm.

But after thinking about Parker as editor of *The Dial* for a few days, he wrote Margaret Fuller on March 21 that he was inclined to undertake the editing of the magazine himself; he preferred to "undertake it alone." Having made the decision, he wrote to contributors to ask for material. He informed Frederic Hedge that he assumed the task "very unwillingly" and only "until a better person appears, more fit for this service & more fond of it." The Spring issue, 1842, had already appeared; the first to be edited by Emerson was the Summer issue of that year. He applied not only to Hedge for contributions, but also to Margaret Fuller, Charles King Newcomb, Jones Very, and Ellery Channing, among others, but felt that, if nothing suitable came in for publication, he could always "rely on . . . a liberal selection of good matter from old or from foreign books."

Despite all his occupation with his lectures, his poetry, the magazine, he kept up his journal. The canker of dissatisfaction gnawed at him from time to time, that necessary goad to the creative spirit. "I have almost completed thirty-nine years, and I have not yet adjusted my relations to my fellows on the planet, or to my own work." A little later, he told Margaret Fuller in the course of a moonlit walk where he saw "the moon broken in the water, interrogating, interrogating," that he "had never been otherwise than indolent, never strained a muscle, and only saw a difference in the circumstance, not in the man" and of his poetry said that his brothers, aunt and cousins "all agreed that my verses were obscure nonsense; and now a larger public say the same

95

thing, 'obscure nonsense,' and yet both conceded that the boy had wit." But of poetry in general, he could write in his journal that it reminded him of the catbird, "who sings so affectedly and vaingloriously to me near Walden. Very sweet and musical! very various! fine execution! but so conscious, and *such a performer!* not a note is his own, except at last, *Miou, miou.*" He admitted, too, that while some people played at chess, or at cards, or the stock exchange, "I prefer to play at Cause and Effect."

He set down, too, an observation which had certainly occurred to many a creative artist in the centuries behind him. "A highly endowed man with good intellect and good conscience is a Man-woman and does not so much need the complement of woman to his being as another. Hence his relations to the sex are somewhat dislocated and unsatisfactory. He asks in woman sometimes the woman, sometimes the man."

When, in June, he took a manuscript by Charles King Newcomb into the woods and "read it in the armchair of the upturned root of a pine tree, [he] felt for the first time since Waldo's death some efficient faith again in the repairs of the Universe, some independency of natural relations whilst spiritual affinities can be so perfect and compensating."

The Dial, while occupying much of his time, did not meet expectations, modest as they were. Emerson had estimated that only 300 subscribers would meet the production cost of $750 for a year's issues, and leave a residue of perhaps $50. There was no lack of contributions. For the first issue under his editorial guidance, Emerson accepted an essay from the redoubtable Arthur Brisbane but felt it necessary to write an introduction to it, discussing Fourier's system, since he did not agree with the imposition of any system "by force of preaching and votes on all men, and carried into rigid execution." Emerson himself contributed a brief statement about student rebellions at Harvard.

Thoreau, who served now and then as assistant to Emerson in his capacity as editor, contributed translations and new poems of his own; Margaret Fuller continued her crusade for women's right's in *The Dial;* Theodore Parker sent in provocative articles about controversial religious subjects; Charles Sterns Wheeler provided letters from Germany; Benjamin Peter Hunt sent in travel sketches. Despite all this, Emerson had to keep his lectures in reserve to fill in with when material fell short of the required number of pages.

Meanwhile, Nathanial Hawthorne, having married Sophia Peabody, came to live in the Old Manse, grandfather Ripley's old house, and the two men saw each other with some frequency, though Hawthorne the man eluded Emerson, and Hawthorne saw more in Emerson's poetry than in his philosophy. They went walking together—sometimes with Thoreau for company. "Our walk had no incidents," recorded Emerson on September 27, 1842. "It needed none, for we were both in excellent spirits, and had much conversation, for we were both old collectors who had never had an opportunity before to show each other our cabinets, so that we could have filled with matter much longer days." They walked on this day "about twenty miles" and next morning continued their walk to Shaker Village and to Acton, and thence back home.

"If a man will kick a fact out of the window," wrote Emerson later that year in his journal, "when he comes back he finds it again in the chimney corner." He was reluctant to accept the fact that *The Dial* could not long survive. Soon it was not even meeting publication costs. Its contributors, who were principally Transcendentalists, brimmed over with optimism—except for Margaret Fuller, who had had enough experience with the magazine to know the difficulties   *97* of keeping it alive; but Transcendentalism was being invaded by Fourierism, and, though its fundamental hope of reconciling science and religion apart from any then known sect remained unchanged, its essential passivity gave way to aggressiveness, and, as the hard facts of economic problems were impressed upon the Transcendentalists, their optimism began to fade. Such a magazine as *The Dial,* though it was held to be necessary reading for the intellectuals of the age, could not expect a very large audience.

Nevertheless, Emerson continued to publicize it, and he had no better opportunity to do so than in the course of his lecture tours. Immediately after Christmas, 1842, he set out on another winter tour, this time to Baltimore, Washington, and Philadelphia, widening his range. Everywhere he spoke of *The Dial* and heard it praised; but in Philadelphia, meeting the antislavery lecturer, Lucretia Mott, he was told tartly that he was "living out of the world." "I was not much flattered," he continued, "that her interest in me respected my rejection of an ordinance sometime somewhere." He wrote Elizabeth Hoar that he was also "challenged on the subject of the Lord's Supper . . . and was forced to recollect the grounds of my dissent."

In Washington he visited the Senate and heard some of the speeches. There he met another disciple, Giles Waldo, who joined his company of correspondents. He watched a lighting experiment by Horatio Greenough. He studied the recently invented telegraph. Wherever he went he took in all the concerts and exhibitions that he could. If he heard anything of *The Dial,* it was all in favor of the magazine; but there was no notable enthusiasm for it, and he did not add very many subscribers through his efforts.

His program that winter was not light, but, what with the failure of some of his investments to pay dividends, he had no recourse but to lecture if he were to pay his debts—among them, the expenses of keeping up *The Dial*. He lectured on New England: "on the Descent, Religion, Trade, Manners, Genius, & recent Spiritual features of the Inhabitants of N. England. Five lectures. (to be read in ten days) 3 evenings in one week 2 in the next," as he wrote to his brother William in a letter proposing to deliver the lectures in New York after he had finished in Philadelphia.

In New York he made the acquaintance of yet another disciple, young William Tappan, who spent some pleasant hours with him, until he "forgot everything but Montaigne & Michel Angelo," he wrote Lidian. He welcomed his disciples, although, as he wrote Margaret Fuller, "I have had so many correspondents lately that I must sometimes appear faithless to the most faithful of all." He wrote her also about *The Dial*, but just before he returned to Concord he heard "good tidings" about the magazine. "It seems," he wrote Lidian, "that we shall quickly see to the end of that labor. For Miss [Elizabeth] Peabody shows me that it no longer pays its expenses, a plain hint from the upper power that it should stop, which I willingly accept."

He returned home early in March and in less than a fortnight wrote Margaret Fuller that he had "many moods concerning the Dial, dependent chiefly, I believe, on those with whom I converse." Though he had made up his mind in the winter of 1843 that *The Dial* must be suspended, his "many moods" kept the magazine alive for another year, for, as he wrote Margaret Fuller in April, he was "unwilling that a book of so good intent & which can avail itself of such costly veins as volunteer to bleed for it, should die."

He plunged again into the routine of life in Concord, which some of his friends thought too passive for him. He watched the growth of Alcott's utopian Fruitlands, another community experiment, and foresaw that it would hardly survive a winter. He observed in his journal, "This fatal fault in the logic of our friends still appears: Their whole doctrine is spiritual, but they always end with saying, Give us much land and money." He was generous in his financial support of Alcott, though he had warned Alcott's English friends that Alcott's "facts" were not so much to be trusted as his theories. But this time, late in 1843, he recorded in his journal that "Transcendentalism is the Saturnalia of faith. It is faith run mad."

Whether or not Concord was provincial, he was now coming to take a wider interest in the problems of the day. Though he was not yet ready to commit himself to an active role in the antislavery movement, he was opposed to slavery. He wrote of Daniel Webster: "He has misused the opportunity of making himself the darling of the American world in all coming time by abstaining from putting himself at the head of the Anti-slavery interest, by standing for New England and for man against the bullying and barbarism of the South." He saw that farming, though it might be "enchanted" labor, was not ultimately rewarding, for "after toiling his brains out, sacrificing thought, religion, taste, love, hope, courage at the shrine of toil, [the farmer] turns out a bankrupt as well as the merchant. It is time to have the thing looked into, and with a transpiercing criticism settled whether life is worth having on such terms."

He was not, however, essentially a man of action. He admitted in his journal that "The capital defect of my nature for society . . . is the want of animal spirits." He invested, albeit cautiously, in the railroad, then making its way toward Concord, but he foresaw that, though "Americans take to the . . . contrivance as if it were the cradle in which they were born," it was also true that "when the rudder is invented for the balloon, railroads will be superseded." He seemed unable to put into practice a more casual routine for guests, though he set down the only sensible course for the treatment of guests: "If we could establish the rule that each man was a guest in his own house, and when we had shown our visitors the passages of the house, the way to fire, to bread, and water, and thus made them as much at home as the inhabitant, did then leave them to the accidents of intercourse, and went about our ordinary business, a guest would no longer be formidable."

Nevertheless, he recorded in his journal with manifest satisfaction: "I enjoy all the hours of my life. Few persons have such susceptibility to pleasure. . . . I never, I think, fear death. It seems to me so often a relief, a rendering-up of responsibility, a quittance of so many vexatious trifles." He walked abroad, he enjoyed the country, he read Ellery Channing's poetry, he listened to Alcott's laments: "Very pathetic it is to see this wandering Emperor from year to year making his round of visits from house to house of such as do not exclude him, seeking a companion, tired of pupils."

The year turned. Fruitlands collapsed, as Emerson had foreseen. He was now at work on the preparation of a second book of essays, and he found himself no different from many another author in the ability to work, noting in his journal: "I never seem well to do a particular work until another is done. I cannot write the poem, though you give me a week, but if I promise to read a lecture day after tomorrow, at once the poem comes into my head and now the rhymes will flow. And let the proofs of the *Dial* be crowding on me from the printer, and I am full of faculty how to make the lecture."

Alcott was forever at his doorstep. Thoreau was at his elbow, ever ready to lend a hand or to argue, as the case might be. He was, as Emerson noted, "the only man of   *101* leisure in the town. . . . He has no troublesome memory, no wake, but lives *ex tempore,* and brings today a new proposition as radical and revolutionary as that of yesterday, but different. . . . I can see that, with his practical faculty, he has declined all the kingdoms of this world."

He began to take a more active interest in the great problems of the day, though he was not yet ready to commit himself. He observed the conservative antagonism to the fresh—and, some thought, dangerously radical—proposals of the more liberal Transcendentalists and concluded, "I think the best argument of the conservative is this bad one: that he is convinced that the angry democrat, who wishes him to divide his park and chateau with him, will, on entering into the possession, instantly become conservative, and hold the property and spend it as selfishly as himself. For a better man, I might dare to renounce my estate; for a worse man, or for as bad a man as I, why should I? All the history of man with unbroken sequence of examples establishes this inference. Yet it is very low and degrading ground to stand upon. We must never reason from history, but plant ourselves on the ideal."

He did not wonder, either, at those feeble men who were strong advocates for slavery. "They have no feeling or worthiness which assures them of their own safety. . . . They live by certain privileges which the actual order of the community yields them. Take those and you take all. . . . fear is very cruel. . . . A gentleman may have many innocent propensities, but if he chances to have the habit of slipping arsenic into the soup of whatever person sits next him at table, he must expect some inconvenience."

During 1844 Emerson enlarged his land holdings and departed from his own writing long enough to translate Dante's *Vita Nuova.* He finally abandoned *The Dial,* having taken a substantial financial loss on the venture in the course of the two years he had edited it. In mid-June he hailed the arrival of the railroad in Concord; actually, locomotives had come through from Boston earlier, but travel did not begin until the seventeenth. He wrote William that "since sunrise the cars have already traversed the distance between our depot & Charlestown 8 times." But an event of greater interest to Emerson loomed.

On July 10, 1844, a second son was born to him. The boy was named Edward Waldo; his birth delighted Emerson, for at last the loss he had felt ever since Waldo's death two years before was diminished—not entirely erased, but lessened.

He was now engrossed in the pending publication of his second collection of essays. He had spent the preceding winter in its preparation, foregoing a lecture tour, and the book was now ready. He devoted all his energies to it, even putting off an urgent appeal from John Greenleaf Whittier to ally himself actively to the Abolitionist cause by attending an antislavery meeting at Acton, however much he approved such meetings being held "& the spirit which they indicate, & which, I doubt not, they spread." He admitted, however, that he was "almost ready to promise you . . . my thought on the best way of befriending the slave & ending slavery."

Having conveyed his book to his publisher, James Munroe & Company in Boston, he sought the woods in the interval before its appearance and "added an absurdity or two to my usual ones," he wrote William. "In one of my solitary wood-walks by Walden Pond, I met two or three men who told me they had come thither to sell & to buy a field, on which they wished me to bid as purchaser. As it was on the shore of the pond, & now for years I had a sort of daily occupancy in it, I bid on it, & bought it, eleven acres for $8.10

per acre." Subsequently he "bought, for 125 dollars more" another piece, "and so am landlord & waterlord of 14 acres, more or less, on the shore of Walden, & can raise my own blackberries."

Essays: Second Series was published in October of that year. It was not quite as imposing a book as the first *Essays*, but it was given a better reception, in part because a large portion of its public had heard most of the essays previously in the form of lectures, though the lectures had been altered and strengthened for book publication. There were nine essays in the book, somewhat casually arranged. They were also rather less Transcendentalist than those in his first book, and it was patent that Emerson drew a little more on his experience and a little less on theory, for he had tried out his theories, and found, as most idealistic theorists invariably discover, that theory is seldom akin to experience, for nothing like experience reveals the flaws in theory.

He led off his volume with *The Poet*, prefacing it, as every other essay in both books, with some lines of verse. He set forth at once his conviction that "the poet is representative. He stands among partial men for the complete man, and appraises us not of his wealth, but of the common wealth." Only the poet, he contended, possesses that "very high sort of seeing, which does not come by study, but by the intellect being where and what it sees," enabling him to make translucid to others the secrets of nature. He alone is the interpreter of nature and the natural mind; he speaks for the universe. This was a theory enunciated long before by Emerson, and applied by him to every creative artist, not only the poet.

Experience, which followed it, proved to be one of the most effective essays in the book, and ought to have been set first. It was perhaps more difficult for Emerson to write than others in the volume because in it theory had to give way to reality. "From the mountain you see the mountain. We animate what we can, and we see only what we animate. . . . Of what use is genius, if the organ is too convex or too concave and cannot find a focal distance within the actual horizon of human life?" he asked.

"That immobility and absence of elasticity which we find in the arts, we find with more pain in men," he complained. In his view, "human life is made up of the two elements, power and form, and the proportion must be invariably kept if we would have it sweet and sound. Each of these elements in excess makes a mischief as hurtful as its defect. Everything runs to excess; every good quality is noxious if unmixed, and, to carry the danger to the edge of ruin, nature causes each man's peculiarity to superabound. . . . The wise through excess of wisdom is made a fool."

He saw that "Illusion, Temperament, Succession, Surface, Surprise, Reality, Subjectiveness—these are threads on the loom of time, these are the lords of life. I dare not assume to give their order, but I name them as I find them in my way." He knew better now, he admitted, "than to claim any completeness for my picture," being himself but a fragment. He could "confidently announce one or another law," but he was "too young yet by some ages to compile a code." Perhaps he might have ventured to do so two decades earlier. In the end, he concluded, "there is victory yet for all justice; and the true romance which the world exists to realize will be the transformation of genius into practical power."

None of the essays in this second volume scintillated like *Self-Reliance* in the first collection; but then, none of the subjects he chose to write about was so close to his core as self-reliance. In *Character*, the third of the essays, he defined his subject as "nature in the highest form. It is of no use to ape it or to contend with it." He was looking on all sides of his subjects as he had not previously done; he was less intent on following his own line to the exclusion of all others. "There are many eyes that can detect and honor the prudent and household virtues," he wrote; "there are many that can discern Genius on his starry track, though the mob is incapable; but when that love which is all-suffering, all-abstaining, all inspiring . . . comes into our streets and houses—only the pure and aspiring can know its fact, and the only compliment they can pay it is to own it."

Emerson could not have written *Manners* without more knowledge of the world in which he lived than he had hitherto revealed in earlier essays. His idealism was clearly being tempered by realism—not so much as to appreciably diminish his optimism, but only so much as to establish a greater rapport with his audience.

Nature was a restatement of the philosophy set forth in his first book of the same name, but one more succinct and one that carried Emerson's awareness of evolution in some of its lines. Nature, he saw now, "publishes itself in creatures, reaching from particles and spiculae through transformation on transformation to the highest symmetries, arriving at consummate results without a shock or a leap. . . . It is a long way from granite to the oyster; farther yet to Plato and the preaching of the immortality of the soul. . . . yet so poor is nature with all her craft, that from the beginning to the end of the universe she has but one stuff—but one stuff with its two ends, to serve up all her dream-like variety. Compound it how she will, star, sand, fire, water, tree, man, it is still one stuff, and betrays the same properties."

One of the most interesting essays in this book was *Politics,* not so much for what it said as for what it left unsaid. There were indications that Emerson, who was considerably more familiar with poverty than with wealth, was ready for reform if not yet ready to make a forthright declaration. It was not an essay to delight the radicals who spoke up for reforms, but just enough of a departure from the acceptance of the *status quo* to make conservative readers uneasy. He pointed out that "too much weight" had been "allowed in the laws to property, and such a structure given to our usages as allowed the rich to encroach on the poor, and to keep them poor." He looked to the highest end "of government" as the "culture of men; and . . . if men can be educated, the institutions will share their improvement and the moral sentiment will write the law of the land."

He declared that "The philosopher, the poet, or the religious man, will of course wish to cast his vote with the democrat, for free-trade, for wide suffrage, for the abolition of legal cruelties in the penal code, and for facilitating in every manner the access of the young and the poor to the sources of wealth and power." Essentially, however, he saw in the most successful government the triumph of the individual; when individuals are improved, the government must also improve. "A man has a right to be employed, to be trusted, to be loved, to be revered"—but the state, however much it tried, could assure no more than employment, for "there will always be a government of force where men are selfish; and when they are pure enough to abjure the code of force they will be wise enough to see how these public ends . . . can be answered."

Had his essay *Politics* been written a year later, it undoubtedly would have been a stronger statement. Only a few weeks before the new collection of essays came off the press, Emerson had at last made a public statement that allied him with the abolition movement when he spoke out in support of emancipation in the West Indies. Since proofing his book, he had also learned, through a visit with William Lloyd Garrison, one of the abolitionist leaders, to take a more benevolent view of the movement.

The new year of 1845 had scarcely begun when the issue of slavery had to be met in Concord itself. Some of the anti-slavery "ladies . . . proposed to contribute to the (Lyceum) course a lecture on Slavery by Wendell Phillips," as he noted in his journal. There had been some opposition, but Emerson "pressed the acceptance on the part of the curators . . . because I thought, in the present state of this country, the particular subject of Slavery had a commanding right to be heard in all places in New England, in season, and sometimes out of reason; that, as in Europe the partition of Poland was an outrage so flagrant that all European men must be willing, once in every month or two, to be plagued with hearing over again the horrid story, so this inquiry of slavery in this country was a ghost that would not down at the bidding of Boston merchants, or the best democratic drill-officers, but the people must consent to be plagued with it from time to time until something was done. . . ." In that same January he took an active part in a Concord meeting called to make an official protest about South Carolina's expulsion of a Massachusetts agent.

He made some further attempt to study Fourier, but in the end discarded Fourierism, and noted in his journal that Thoreau said of the Fourierists that they "had a sense of duty which led them to devote themselves to their second best." He was disturbed by the annexation of Texas, which struck him as "one of those events which retard or retrograde the civilization of ages," but he admitted that "the World Spirit is a good swimmer, and storms and waves cannot easily drown him." He bought land for Alcott's use, while some of Alcott's relatives bought him a house, but reflected that Alcott "should be made effective by being tapped by a good suction-pump."

Slavery as an institution repelled him more and more, and he became more concerned. His journal, which had been neglected for much of the previous year, reflected his increased preoccupation. "What argument, what eloquence can avail against the power of that one word *niggers*? The man of the world annihilates the whole combined force of all the anti-slavery societies of the world by pronouncing it," he wrote. The question of slavery, he recorded, "has never been presented to the South with a kind and thoroughly scientific treatment, as a question of pure political economy in the largest sense."

Late that spring, when Thoreau wanted to withdraw from Concord for the purpose of making an experiment in the economy of living, to see how cheaply a man could live, Emerson allowed him to build a hut on his land on Walden Pond; and, after Thoreau had gone there in July to live, and Emerson saw how well this reclusive hut suited him, set forth in a new will he made that Thoreau was to inherit hut and land at Emerson's death.

That summer he went on a lecture tour, arousing some critical comment by the increasingly radical nature of his lectures. He was again the object of attack by clergymen, both at Middlebury College in Vermont and at Wesleyan University in Connecticut, where he was charged with heresy. He refused, however, to lecture at New Bedford because Negroes were not permitted to become members of the lyceum in that city. By December, 1845, though he had begun the work of collecting a volume of his poems, he began a new series of lectures for the Boston Lyceum, this time on representative men, a sequence of biographical studies dealing with Plato, Montaigne, Shakespeare, Goethe, and others, seven in all. The new series proved to be as successful financially as any he had done. He repeated the lectures at Lowell and some other towns and then returned to Concord to take up his projected book of poems.

He worked at its preparation all during the remainder of 1846, but suffered many interruptions. He helped raise money to send Ellery Channing to visit Europe. He spoke out against the Mexican War. He was not much impressed by Thoreau's going to jail rather than paying his poll tax for the support of a government that would tolerate such an institution as slavery; he thought that sitting in prison did not get to the heart of the matter and was too passive a protest, either against slavery or the Mexican War. "The Abolitionists denounce the war," he noted in his journal, "and give much time to it, but they pay the tax." He observed, too, that the "rabble at Washington are really better than the snivelling opposition. They have a sort of genius of a bold and manly cast, though Satanic. They see, against the unanimous expression of the people, how much a little well-directed effrontery can achieve, how much crime the people will bear, and they proceed from step to step."

Work on the manuscript went steadily ahead. "The writer must live and die by his writing," reflected Emerson. "Good for that, and good for nothing else." As for his increasing involvement in the world, he was bound to admit, "I like man, but not men. . . . The etiquette of society should guard and consecrate a poet; he should not be visited, nor be shown at dinner-tables: too costly to be seen except on high holidays. He should be relieved of visits and trivial correspondence. His time is the time of his nation."

The book, titled *Poems,* made its appearance late in December of that year, though the printer's notice had it 1847. The arrangement of the poems, from the reader's point of view, left something to be desired, for the poems most readily comprehended and likely to please were well to the rear, and the more difficult, more formidable poems came at the beginning of the volume. *The Rhodora, The Humble-Bee,* and *Concord Hymn*—all already popular with the audience previously familiar with them—were placed behind such longer and more difficult poems as *The Sphinx, Uriel,* and *The Problem.*

For all that the book was indifferently received, principally because of Emerson's emphasis on introspective philosophy, it was nevertheless an important publication, for Emerson's verse was central to the development of American poetry from his time onward. It paid little homage to tradition. Though his lines were usually firm and strong, Emerson was not much concerned with the traditional forms. He placed the first emphasis on what he had to say, and less on metre and rhythm; he was only incidentally interested in perfection of a rhyme pattern, and ideology took precedence over sentiment.

The leading poem particularly puzzled readers. Thoreau labored for hours over the meaning of *The Sphinx* and gave it up at last, far from Emerson's own later explanation: "The perception of identity unites all things and explains one by another, and the most rare and strange is equally facile as the most common. But if the mind live only in particulars, and see only differences (wanting the power to see the whole—all in each), then the world addresses to this mind a question it cannot answer, and each new fact tears it in pieces, and it is vanquished by the distracting variety." Small wonder that many a reader failed to get past *The Sphinx!*

Emerson, however, was pleased with the book. "I am free at last of my little white book" (it was bound in a white binding), he wrote his brother William late in 1846, "whose fate the readers may now settle. I have just now been writing a new paper on 'Eloquence,' which interests me. . . ."

Readers did not flock to buy the little volume, but at least one reviewer was aware of its merit, and wrote in the *Boston Courier* as if with some intimation of the influence Emerson's verse was to have upon poets in America, calling it "one of the most peculiar and original volumes of poetry ever published in the United States."

I suppose that liberty is an accurate index,
in men and nations, of general progress. The
theory of personal liberty must always
appeal to the most refined communities
and to the men of the rarest perception and
of delicate moral sense. For there are rights
which rest on the finest sense of justice, and,
with every degree of civility, it will be more
truly felt and defined. A barbarous tribe of
good stock will, by means of their best
heads, secure substantial liberty. But where
there is any weakness in a race, and it
becomes in a degree matter of concession
and protection from their stronger
neighbors, the incompatibility and
offensiveness of the wrong will of course
be most evident to the most cultivated. For
it is—is it not?—the essence of courtesy, of
politeness, of religion, of love, to prefer
another, to postpone oneself, to protect
another from oneself. That is the distinction
of the gentleman, to defend the weak and
redress the injured, as it is of the savage
and the brutal to usurp and use others.
      The Fugitive Slave Law

L ate in 1846, Emerson had received an invitation to deliver his lectures in England, and as 1847 came in, he was considering acceptance, though with no great confidence that he would be well received on the lecture platform abroad. Chapman's publication of *Poems* in England had renewed interest in the author of *Essays,* and the suggestion had been made by Alexander Ireland, his old friend of his Edinburgh visit in 1833, that the time was right for an extensive tour of England and Scotland. At first Emerson would give no definite answer, but at least he did not reject the suggestion, even though Carlyle soon added his support to Ireland's suggestion.

While the matter simmered, Emerson became involved in the publication of a successor to *The Dial,* and was announced as "in the Direction" of *The Massachusetts Quarterly Review,* somewhat to his annoyance, and found it necessary to prepare an editorial for the first issue. As the spring wore on, he planted an extensive orchard, principally 128 pear and apple trees, after which, he brought young pine trees from his Walden property and transplanted them around his home. Then, with Thoreau and Alcott, he cut hemlock trees with which Alcott and Thoreau presently built him a summer house he called Tumbledown Hall.

CHAPTER 9

The American Genius

By midsummer, Emerson had decided to chance lecturing abroad. He had been stimulated by a critical essay written by the Countess Marie de Flavigny d'Agoult and published in *La Review indépendante* for July 25, 1846, in which he had been called a profoundly wise man beholden to no nature but his own and an authentic American genius, impatient with tradition. Even while he was now making ready for his tour abroad, the French critic Emile Montégut, writing in the *Revue des deux mondes*, hailed his originality of thought and his unswerving devotion to truth, and put him in the same company as Montaigne. Both studies were influential in shaping public opinion and arousing curiosity as to what manner of man Emerson might be.

He sailed out of Boston on the *Washington Irving* on October 5 and landed at Liverpool on October 22. After meeting with Ireland, he made his way to London to visit Carlyle. "We had a wide talk that night until nearly one o'clock, and at breakfast next morning again. At noon or later we walked forth to Hyde Park, and the palaces, about two miles from here, to the National Gallery, and to the Strand, Carlyle melting all Westminster and London into his talk and laughter. . . ." He decided anew that Carlyle was "not mainly a scholar, like the most of my acquaintances, but a very practical Scotchman, such as you would find in any saddler's or iron-dealer's shop, and then only accidentally and by a surprising addition the admirable scholar and writer he is."

At Manchester and Liverpool he delivered such lectures as *Domestic Life, Reading,* and the *Representative Men* he had inaugurated at the Boston Lyceum. There was no dearth of requests for him to lecture—more, in fact, than he could accept; he left it to Ireland to select those engagements he ought to fill: but he wrote Lidian early in December that his "reception here is rather dubious & by no means so favorable as

Henry pleases to fancy. I am preached against every Sunday by the Church of England, & by the Church of Swedenborg, and [by] the Athenaeum & the Examiner newspaper denounced . . . for letting in such a wolf into the English fold."

He wrote his wife, too, of his distress at the sight of waifs begging in the streets of Manchester and Liverpool. "My dearest little Edie, to tell you the truth, costs me many a penny, day by day. I cannot go up the street but I shall see some woman in rags with a little creature just of Edie's age & size, but in coarsest ragged clothes, & barefooted, stepping beside her, and I look curiously into *her* Edie's face, with some terror lest it should resemble *mine, and* the far-off Edie wins from me the halfpence for this near one."

He went on from Manchester after Christmas to lecture in Worcester, Leeds, Halifax, Ripon, Sheffield and York—for the most part on the representative men he had chosen. After a fortnight's respite, he went to Scotland to lecture in Edinburgh and Glasgow. He was widely attacked by the conservatives, and hailed by the liberals, as perhaps he expected; but in all there was about him that kind of publicity that brought him to the attention of the people who might and did come to listen to him. Silence would have served the conservatives better, but their opposition served him well, for it made him seem to be the apostle of democracy, the spirit of which was even then stirring beneath the surface all over Europe, to erupt in that very year, 1848.

He used his time well. He went to exhibitions and concerts; he accepted invitations to visit at private homes; he heard other lecturers, among them Sir William Hamilton ("the great man of the college"); he called on fellow writers, among them Thomas De Quincey ("a small old man of 70 years, with a very handsome face, and a face too expressing the highest refinement, a very gentle old man, speaking with the greatest deliberation & softness, and so refined in speech & manners as to make quite indifferent his extremely plain & poor dress"), Mrs. Catherine Crowe ("a very distinguished good person here"), and others; he sat for his portrait by David Scott.

After lecturing at Dundee, Perth, and Paisley, Emerson went to visit the writer Harriet Martineau, and from there called on William Wordsworth. Soon he was in London once more, living in the Strand. He was much in demand there and late in March wrote Lidian a long letter about the hospitality accorded him. "I have seen a great many people and some very good ones." They were writers, actors, aristocrats, bishops; they included men like Richard Owen ("who is in England what Agassiz is in America"), Thomas Babington Macaulay ("He has the strength of ten men; immense memory, fun, fire, learning, politics, manners, & pride,—talks all the time in a steady torrent"), and Henry Hallam ("quiet & affable & courteous"). There was little of London that he missed, from government leaders and aristocrats to paupers, and everywhere that spring the conversation was of the revolution taking place in France. Before leaving London he met Matthew Arnold, Charles Dickens, and Alfred, Lord Tennyson ("tall, scholastic-looking, no dandy, but a great deal of plain strength about him, and though cultivated, quite unaffected; quiet, sluggish sense and strength, refined, as all English are, and good-humoured. There is in him an air of general superiority, that is very satisfactory").

He went on to Paris and found himself in the thick of the revolution. He saw Rachel in several plays and found that Paris, even in revolt, pleased him more than at his first visit a decade and a half earlier. "Paris has great merits as a city," he wrote in his journal. "Its river is made the greatest pleasure to the eye by the quays and bridges; its fountains are noble and copious; its gardens or parks far more available to the pleasure of the people than those of London. . . . the living is cheap and good. . . . The manners of the people are full of entertainment, so spirited, chatty, and coquettish, as lively as monkeys. . . . The cafés are not to be forgotten, filled with newspapers, blazing with light, sauntering places, *oubliettes* or remember-nothings."

Returning to England, he was prevailed upon to lecture in London, visited the British Museum again under the guidance of Coventry Patmore and Sir Charles Fellowes, went again to the opera, attended a meeting of the Geological Society of London, and found himself again charged with obscurity in his lectures. He went to visit Stonehenge with Carlyle, visited Charles Bray at Coventry, spent some time with Mary Ann Evans (George Eliot), and then, with Arthur Hugh Clough, went to Liverpool in mid-July to embark for home. He reached his native shores late in July of that year.

The European sojourn had broadened him. Witnessing the French Revolution had sharpened his awareness. Life, he had written a year earlier, "consists in what a man is thinking all day," and now he was thinking of more than his acres, his books, his family. He had set down at the same time the "Superstitions of our Age: The fear of Catholicism; The fear of pauperism; The fear of immigration; The fear of manufacturing interests; The fear of radicalism or democracy; And faith in the steam engine." But already some of these superstitions had taken on new meaning. At home he could not escape the pressures of the age, for Concord was no provincial village, it lay not far from Boston, and all events revolving about that city touched upon Concord.

He tried to submerge himself in his affairs. He bought still more land, he worked in his garden, though he admitted that "God never made such a bungler as I am at any practical work, therefore I keep clear of the garden and the phalan-stery." His children were ever present and dear to him, and they served to temper his philosophy still more with reality.

At the same time, he was finding less satisfaction in his old companions, though he spent no less time with them. "Alcott," he observed in his journal, "is a man of unquestionable genius, yet no doctrine or sentence or word or action of his which is excellent can be detached and quoted." He set down Thoreau's verdict of Alcott as "the best natured man I ever met. The rats and mice make their nests in him," even while recording that Thoreau was "like the wood-god who solicits the wandering poet and draws him into antres vast and des-arts [sic] idle, and bereaves him of his memory, and leaves him naked, plaiting vines and with twigs in his hand." He walked out at least twice a week with Ellery Channing—to Conantum or Walden and wondered "where is he who is to save the present moment, and cause that this beauty be not lost?"

His delight in nature was not diminished by his growing concern about the institution of slavery. "My wood lot has no price," he admitted in a journal entry. "I could not think of selling it for the money I gave for it. It is full of unknown mysterious values. What forms, what colours, what powers, null, it is true, to our ignorance, but opening inestimably to human wit. The crows filled the landscape with a savage sound; the ground was covered with new fallen leaves which rustled so loud as we trampled through them that we could hear nothing else."

Late in 1848, and throughout the winter of 1849, he was once more on the lecture circuit through New England and in Philadelphia, New York, Brooklyn, and other eastern cities. This time he lectured frequently on England and also gave *Natural Aristocracy,* which he had first given in Edinburgh.

His tour was so successful that he cleared $630 above expenses, for the city lectures alone.

At home again, he got to work on manuscripts. He prepared a reprint of *Nature* together with addresses and lectures for publication later in 1849, and began to assemble *Representative Men*. "Like the New England soil," he wrote in his journal, "my talent is good only whilst I work it. If I cease to task myself, I have no thoughts. This is a poor sterile Yankeeism. What I admire and love is the generous and spontaneous soil which flowers and fruits at all seasons." His obligations in his home were onerous from time to time. "Duties are as much impediments to greatness as cares. If a man sets out to be rich, he cannot follow his genius; neither can he any more, if he wishes to be an estimable son, brother, husband, nephew, and cousin."

Representative Men appeared early in 1850. The reprint of *Nature* had appeared the preceding September, followed by a reprint of the second series of *Essays*. But *Representative Men*, though it was familiar to his lecture audiences, had not previously appeared in book form, and for publication all the lectures had been extensively revised. His "representative" men illustrated ideas, rather than led heroic lives; he saw in them the kind of self-reliance he himself vaunted. His Plato was as much a mystic as he himself, and so was Swedenborg, in spite of what Emerson called his "theological bias." He still praised, as he had always done, the wisdom of Montaigne, in whose work "the moral sentiment" never forfeited its supremacy. He tended to apply Transcendentalist standards to all his representative men, including Shakespeare and Goethe, not quite successfully.

While individual essays in the new book fanned old controversies, the book itself did not disturb readers nearly as much as its predecessors. It was quickly pirated and widely sold in England, where James A. Froude, reviewing it in *The Eclectic Review,* suggested that Emerson ought to be telling readers about his own countrymen, rather than the Europeans. But in general the attitude of critics and reviewers was that Emerson's best work lay behind him.

"The English journals snub my new book," he wrote in his journal, "as, indeed, they have all its foregoers. Only now they say that this has less vigor and originality than the others. Where, then, was the degree of merit that entitled my books to their notice? They have never admitted the claims of either of them. The fate of my books is like the impression of my face. My acquaintances, as long back as I can remember, have always said, 'Seems to me you look a little thinner than when I saw you last.' "

But he could not be troubled about reviews or the lack of them. Within a short time after publication of *Representative Men* he was again on the lecture circuit. This time he went far from New England. He accepted engagements as far west as Cincinnati, Ohio, where he earned enough money to justify a venture into the Mississippi Valley. From Cincinnati he went to visit Mammoth Cave, Kentucky, which cost him a week, as he wrote Lidian, giving her a detailed description of the cave. Then he took a stage back to the Cumberland River, and went on by boat to Paducah. On the steamboat *Washington* he traveled to St. Louis, where he spent three days before he moved up "the broad, lonely, islanded, lake-like" Mississippi to Galena. He had planned to go north as far as the Falls of St. Anthony to sit and watch the council of Indians there, but, learning that the council was over, he chose instead to leave Galena by stage for Elgin, "across nearly the whole state of Illinois one measureless prairie." From Chicago he moved steadily back to Massachusetts, reaching home, as he wrote William, "an hour before my letter to Lidian dated St. Louis."

He had returned early in July, and within three weeks learned that his old friend and correspondent, Margaret Fuller, who in Italy had married the Marquis of Ossoli, had died with her husband and their child when their ship the *Elizabeth,* returning from Italy, had foundered on the rocks of Fire Island. He immediately dispatched Thoreau "to go on all our parts," as he wrote Horace Greeley, "& obtain on the wrecking ground all the intelligence &, if possible, any fragments of manuscript or other property."

In his journal he wrote: "To the last her country proves inhospitable to her; brave, eloquent, subtle, accomplished, devoted, constant soul! If Nature availed in America to give birth to many such as she, freedom and honour and letters and art too were safe in this New World. She had great tenderness and sympathy. . . ." Thoreau's search was in vain, and Emerson wrote to his brother William, "Would it not be better that the United States, instead of keeping troops in forts, should keep a coast-guard at lighthouses & wrecking grounds, to defend the lives & properties of mariners from wreckers?"

Greeley's reaction was that a biographical memoir of Margaret Fuller Ossoli must be got ready, and that Emerson must do it. Somewhat to his reluctance, Emerson agreed and began to work slowly with several collaborators to bring the book into being, though it was not until February, 1852, that the *Memoirs of Margaret Fuller Ossoli* appeared in two volumes, very much the work of Emerson, who had permitted most of her story to be told in excerpts from her own writing, adding only comments of his own.

In the winter of 1850–51 he went again on his usual lecture

tour—at first in New England, then Buffalo, then as far west as Pittsburgh. He was now delivering a lecture series entitled *Conduct of Life,* and the western audiences hailed him as the champion of eastern culture.

But a new lecture that was essentially a statement of position was taking shape in his mind. He had been aroused as never before by the passage of various compromise measures, based on resolutions offered by Senator Henry Clay, intended to allay some of the conflict over slavery. He was particularly outraged by the Fugitive Slave Law of September 18, 1850, which provided a fine or imprisonment for any citizen who aided an escaping slave or who obstructed his recapture. And he was incensed at Daniel Webster's support of the compromise measures and declared himself irrevocably in support of Massachusetts's Charles Sumner, who opposed them.

"All I have and all I can do shall be given and done in opposition to the execution of the law," he wrote in his journal, referring to the Fugitive Slave Law specifically. "Since Webster's speech . . . all the interim has really been a period of calamity to New England. That was a steep step downward. I had praised the tone and attitude of the country. My friends had mistrusted it. They say now, It is no worse than it was before; only it is manifest and acted out. Well I think *that* worse. It shows the access of so much courage in the bad, so much check of virtue, terror of virtue, withdrawn. The tameness is shocking. . . .

"The word *liberty* in the mouth of Mr. Webster sounds like the word *love* in the mouth of a courtezan. The little fact comes out more plainly that you cannot rely on any man for the defence of truth who is not constitutionally on that side. . . . It will be his distinction to have changed in one day, by the most detestable law that was ever enacted by a civi-

lized state, the fairest and most triumphant national es-
cutcheon the sun ever shone upon. . . .

"This filthy enactment was made in the nineteenth century,
by people who could read and write. I will not obey it, by
God." The Fugitive Slave Law, he was convinced, must be
done away with, and so, too, the entire institution of slavery.
"Root it out, burn it up, pay for the damage, and let us have
done with it."

His first public address on the subject of the Fugitive Slave
Law was made in Concord on May 3, 1851. Citizens of Concord had for some time aided in the escape of fugitive slaves
and were in no mood to change. His address was made from
the perspective of Massachusetts and the part played by his
native state in the cause against slavery. He attacked the in-
famous law, but though, as he had written, "Union is a de-
lectable thing, and so is wealth, and so is life, but they may
all cost too much, if they cost honour," he advocated no destruction of the union. Rather, he fell back upon what the
British had done in the West Indies, which he had so praised
in his earlier address on that subject, and suggested that the
government might buy all the slaves, no matter what the cost.
The money could be raised by special taxes such as a chimney tax, and by the melting down of church plate and the
sacrifice of some of their wealth by the rich.

He repeated his address throughout Middlesex County in
the support of a candidate for congress on the Free Soil
ticket. He delivered it at Cambridge, where as was heckled by
Harvard students, who broke into his address with cheers for
Webster and Clay, but Emerson was not to be routed; he
stood his ground and waited for his hecklers to finish, then
went on.

Having gone so far, however, he paused. His abolitionist   125

friends wished him to go on. Lucretia Mott, hailing his statement, tried to persuade him to lecture against slavery in
Philadelphia. He would not. He had gone as far for the time
being as he could. He also had some doubts about the rising
tide of women's rights, which kept him from going all the way
into the liberal camp. He noted in his journal, on the occasion
of a women's convention at Worcester, that they were "not
on the right footing . . . as long as they have not equal rights
of property and right of voting," and that such a convention
could not "much avail."

He made some attempt to resume his routine, reading
Goethe and holding him to be "the pivotal man of the old
and new times with us," scoring Thoreau for his want of
ambition—"instead of being the head of American engineers,
he is captain of a huckleberry party"—mourning, on a ramble
with Thoreau, "the eternal loneliness. How insular and pathe-
tically solitary are all the people we know."

He went off again, as winter came on, to lecture, repeating
his lecture series entitled *Conduct of Life* in Boston, going
north as far as Montreal, where he was very popular because
he spoke on Anglo-American relations. He was beginning to
find, however, that the newspapers were reporting so much
of his speeches as to make it difficult for him to offer his
audiences something new. He wrote to Elizur Wright, editor
of the Boston *Commonwealth*, that "your reporter does all he
can to kill the thing to every hearer, by putting him in possession beforehand of the words of each statement that struck
him, as nearly as he could copy them. Abuse me, & welcome,
but do not transcribe me."

But his position on slavery troubled him, nevertheless. "I
waked at night," he wrote in his journal in the summer of
1852, "and bemoaned myself, because I had not thrown myself into this deplorable question of Slavery, which seems to

want nothing so much as a few assured voices." His actions, however, limited as they were, were on the side of the liberals. He bought Hungarian bonds that spring and introduced Louis Kossuth, the Hungarian leader, to his townsmen. He donated to the cause of a fugitive slave in whose welfare Thoreau was interested. At Webster's death late in October, Emerson in his journal recorded that "Nature had not in our days, or not since Napoleon, cut out such a masterpiece. . . . But alas! he was the victim of his ambition; to please the South betrayed the North, and was thrown out by both."

He could not easily yield to the continuing entreaties by Wendell Phillips and Lucretia Mott and others to lecture at the Pennsylvania Anti-Slavery Fair in December, for he was once again on the lyceum platform, delivering a series of lectures, and the winter of 1852–53 took him again to St. Louis and into Illinois to speak on a tour that was financially highly successful, for it earned him over one thousand dollars, and prompted him—following the death of his mother, Ruth Haskins Emerson, in November, 1853—to repeat and expand his western tour, this time going into Michigan and Wisconsin.

That spring of 1854 he was aroused anew in the antislavery cause by the passage of the Kansas-Nebraska Bill, which effectively annulled the Missouri Compromise by guaranteeing Federal nonintervention in the territories. He began to denounce it from the time of its introduction in Congress in March, and it had not yet passed when he took the occasion of the anniversary of Webster's speech in support of Clay's compromise resolutions to speak again, this time in New York, on the Fugitive Slave Law.

He began by admitting that he did not speak often on public questions: "they are odious and hurtful, and it seems like meddling or leaving your work." He admitted that he had never suffered any "known inconvenience" from the institution of slavery. "I never felt the check on my free speech and action, until . . . Mr. Webster, by his personal influence, brought the Fugitive Slave Law on the country. . . . though the bill was not his . . . he was the life and soul of it . . . and under the shadow of his great name inferior men sheltered themselves, threw their ballots for it and made the law."

Once more he stressed the importance of self-reliance both in individual and national life. The word *slave*, he pointed out, did not appear in the constitution, which would "not warrant the crimes that are done under it." He declared that "If slavery is good, then is lying, theft, arson, homicide, each and all good, and to be maintained by Union societies." He ended by supporting unequivocally the Anti-Slavery Society, "the Cassandra that has foretold all that has befallen," and hoped that "we have reached the end of our unbelief, have come to a belief that there is a divine Providence in the world, which will not save us but through our own cooperation."

His address was well received, but it lacked the fighting spirit, and the ringing phrases that the abolitionist movement demanded. He recognized that his address suffered for the want of spirit and the abundance of philosophy, and he knew that he was at his best as an uncommitted observer. Moreover, activity on behalf of any cause—particularly the activity his abolitionist friends asked of him—was not only foreign to his nature, but violated his deepest need, as he set it forth in his journal after his Fugitive Slave Law address in 1854: "If Minerva offered me a gift and an option, I would say give me continuity." He meant to keep his hand in the fight, but no more.

. . . the necessity of solitude is deeper than we have said, and is organic. I have seen many a philosopher whose world is large enough for only one person. . . . A man must be clothed with society, or we shall feel a certain bareness and poverty, as of a displaced and unfurnished member. Now and then a man exquisitely made can live alone, and must; but coop up most men and you undo them. . . . A higher civility will reestablish in our customs a certain reverence which we have lost. . . . Solitude is impracticable, and society fatal. We must keep our head in the one and our hands in the other. . . . It is not the circumstance of seeing more or fewer people, but the readiness of sympathy, that imports; and a sound mind will derive its principles from insight, with ever a purer ascent to the sufficient and absolute right, and will accept society as the natural element in which they are to be applied.

Society and Solitude

After yet another lecture tour in the winter of 1854–55, Emerson settled down again in Concord, making only local appearances or giving occasional addresses not far away. He read widely, but with less enthusiasm, and it was not until that summer than he read a book he liked uncommonly. This was Walt Whitman's *Leaves of Grass.*

Earlier in that year he had written in his journal, "I trust a good deal to common fame, as we all must. If a man has good corn, or wood, or boards, or pigs, to sell, or can make better chairs or knives, crucibles or church organs, than anybody else, you will find a broad hard-beaten road to his house, though it be in the woods." Now he recognized in Whitman a soul as free as his own—indeed, perhaps more free, with less care for conventions and traditions than he, and with no need for that continuity so dear to Emerson. He could not have avoided seeing the similarity between Whitman's ideas and his own so frequently set down in the essays and lectures. Whitman wrote what was implicit in much of Emerson's work: "I do not trouble my spirit to vindicate itself or be understood.... elementary laws never apologize.... Apart from the pulling and hauling stands what I am...." And what had Emerson done for much of his life but "loaf and invite" his soul?

CHAPTER 10

A Higher Civility

He had received his copy of *Leaves of Grass* from Whitman himself, since it was now generally acknowledged that Emerson was the most influential American literary man. He could hardly have hoped that Emerson's response would have been as generous and enthusiastic as it was. Emerson read the book with growing delight, though not without some qualm at Whitman's frank avowals of sexual pleasure and what seemed to him an earthy animalism that informed the poems. His enthusiasm overcame any doubt he might have had about the impression the poems might make on the wider audience he himself had reached, and he wrote Whitman a brief but perceptive letter saluting him.

"I am not blind to the worth of the wonderful gift of *Leaves of Grass*. I find it the most extraordinary piece of wit and wisdom that America has yet contributed. I am very happy in reading it, as great power makes us happy. It meets the demand I am always making of what seemed the sterile & stingy nature, as if too much handiwork or too much lymph in the temperament were making our western wits fat & mean. I give you joy of your free & brave thought. I have great joy in it. I find incomparable things said incomparably well, as they must be. I find the courage of treatment, which so delights me, & which large perception only can inspire. I greet you at the beginning of a great career, which yet must have had a long foreground somewhere, for such a start. I rubbed my eyes a little to see if this sunbeam were no illusion; but the solid sense of the book is a sober certainty. It has the best merits, namely, of fortifying & encouraging."

Whitman shared the same vision Emerson had, and Emerson recognized it at once. Yet his espousal of *Leaves of Grass* dismayed many of his friends and disconcerted the critics. While Emerson praised Whitman's achievement in letters to his friends, readers were repelled by the frankness of the poems and were unable to understand his sponsorship. When Emerson's letter of praise was published, some readers thought it a forgery and demanded his assurance that he had indeed written it. Emerson was somewhat surprised to find his letter in print, at first in the New York *Tribune,* then in a pamphlet, but he would not disavow it or retreat in any way from his praise, though he admitted to Moncure Conway, a young radical disciple, that, had he known his letter would be published, he might have rephrased it.

He met Whitman in New York late that year, as he was preparing for his usual lecture tour, and the two men began an uneasy friendship that endured for years. He was now on his way west once again, into a winter of extreme cold. He wrote Lidian of it and set down in his journal, at Beloit, Wisconsin, early in January, 1856: "This climate and people are a new test for the wares of a man of letters. All his thin, watery matter freezes; 'tis only the smallest portion of alcohol that remains good."

His lectures increased his fame and his many appearances helped to sell his books. Indeed, his lectures ultimately became his books, and his appearance on the platform had prepared an audience for them. His fame was now such that his career was surveyed in journals of the day, and translations of critical notices published abroad were circulated. Theodore Parker, writing in *The Massachusetts Quarterly Review,* said of him that he was at one and the same time the most American and the most cosmopolitan of writers. Whatever the shortcomings of Emerson's scholarship, Parker hailed him as among the foremost geniuses the nation had so far brought forth. Arthur Clough, after returning to England from a visit to America, thought Emerson "the only profound man" in the United States.

He was now working at the manuscript of another book, *English Traits*, made up from the lectures on England he had given some years before, while he gave such popular lectures as *Beauty*. Some of the chapters of the book had already been sent to the publisher, though the book itself did not appear until August, 1856. He had worked on it ever since his visit to England in 1848, and it had grown to respectable size; but his long period of work on it had made of it an unusually unified book.

English Traits was an objective view of the country and its people, written primarily out of his own observation. It was immediately popular both in his native country and in England; within a month the book had sold three thousand copies and had been reprinted. The demand for his books remained constant. Both volumes of *Essays* were reprinted in 1856, and a fifth printing of the *Poems* made its appearance.

English readers of the new book were generally agreed that Emerson's appraisal of England and the English people was just and generous—more so than Nathaniel Hawthorne, then serving as consul in Liverpool, would credit. Carlyle and Clough wrote Emerson in praise of it, and yet the book was no unalloyed paean of praise, but such a judicious balance between praise and criticism as to excite the admiration of its readers, English or American.

At home Emerson found his old pleasures the most satisfying. He was amused at Thoreau's industry when he visited the Sawmill Brook with him one day in May. "He was in search of yellow violets (*pubescens*) and *menyanthes* which he waded into the water for; and which he concluded, on examination, had been out five days. Having found his flowers, he drew out of his breast pocket his diary and read the names of all the plants that should bloom this day . . . whereof he keeps account as a banker when his notes fall due; *Rubus triflora, Quercus, Vaccinium,* etc. The *Cypri-*

pedium not due till tomorrow. . . . He thinks he could tell by the flowers what day of the month it is, within two days."

He attended meetings for the relief of Kansas, now embattled between pro- and antislavery settlers, and contributed to the cause; he went with his family to Pigeon Cove for a holiday; he reflected that "There are men who as soon as they are born take a bee-line to the axe of the inquisitor." He attended the monthly meetings of the Saturday Club, which he had helped bring into being, and which included among its members many leading lights of Boston and environs—Louis Agassiz, the scientist then tutoring pupils, among them Ellen Emerson; Richard Henry Dana; James Russell Lowell; and others, who provided sprightly and challenging debate. He spoke on occasion about the burning question of slavery, and found himself everywhere cast among the angels, and held up as an abolitionist, albeit not a very zealous one.

In January he was on his way to lecture in the Middle West again. He traveled from Syracuse to Rochester with Horace Greeley, who "rose at 6, lit the candles, & scribbled political paragraphs to send away to the Tribune. He is an admirable editor, but I had as lief travel with an Express or with Barnum," he wrote Lidian. He gave lectures: *Beauty, Poetry, The Scholar, France, Life.* In Chicago he learned about land values in that city from W. B. Ogden, who had in one year sold at a million dollars land he had bought for a tenth of that sum. One of his listeners in Madison, Wisconsin, sent a letter to Concord after him with some philosophy of his own in it—"the secret of drunkenness is, that it insulates us in thought, whilst it unites us in feeling."

His routine now was settled and basically unchanged from year to year. He was everywhere in demand as a lecturer, and he gave his winters to lecturing. The rest of the year he spent reading, writing, socializing—to a lesser extent, walking in the environs of Concord. There was little variation in the general course of his existence that his journal did not reflect.

In the course of 1857 "Captain John Brown of Kansas," whom Emerson had met through Thoreau, "gave a good account of himself in the Town Hall, last night, to a meeting of citizens" that included Emerson. "One of his good points was, the folly of the peace party in Kansas, who believed that their strength lay in the greatness of their wrongs, and so discountenanced resistance." Emerson was favorably impressed with Brown's argument supporting forceful resistance.

In that same year he contributed *Days,* one of his more successful poems, to the first issue of *The Atlantic Monthly,* edited by James Russell Lowell. He had the remains of his mother and Waldo removed to the Sleepy Hollow Cemetery ("Waldo's was well preserved—now fifteen years. I ventured to look into the coffin"). He spent long hours in the woods, as one July day he went with Ellery Channing "on the river. A sky of Calcutta; light, air, clouds, water, banks, birds, grass, pads, lilies, were in perfection, and it was delicious to live." He reflected that "To teach us the first lesson of humility, God set man down in these two vastitudes of Space and Time, yet is he such an incorrigible peacock that he thinks them only a perch to show his dirty feathers on."

Emerson was now no longer a member of any church. He had legally separated himself from formal religion of any kind, but, to satisfy Lidian, he continued to support the church. He was at last openly practicing what he had preached for many years, and had done with any mediation between God and himself.

But he was now convinced that his power as a writer was failing. "I am a natural reader, and only a writer in the absence of natural writers," he set down in his journal. "In a true time, I should never have written." In spring, 1859, he wrote, "I have been writing and speaking what were once called novelties, for twenty-five or thirty years, and have not now one disciple . . . because what I said did not go from any wish in me to bring men to me, but to themselves. . . . This is my boast that I have no school follower. I should account it a measure of the impurity of insight, if it did not create independence."

His brother Bulkeley, after living half a century in his retarded state, finally died in 1859, and Emerson saw him buried at Concord. Less than two months later he was himself invalided by a sprain suffered when he came down from the summit of Little Wachusett; he was impatient with the doctors who tried to hasten his cure. He did not permit his sprained foot to keep him from delivering an address at a dinner for Oliver Wendell Holmes on the occasion of Holmes's fiftieth birthday.

When John Brown attacked Harpers Ferry and was captured, Emerson lamented. He reminded his brother William that Brown had been "our guest twice." He called him "a true hero" but believed that at Harpers Ferry Brown had "lost his head." He saluted him in a lecture titled *Courage,* which he delivered on November 8, 1859, in Boston, and took part on December 2, the day of Brown's execution, in a memorial he had planned with Alcott and Thoreau in Concord.

His lameness did not prevent him from going west again early in 1860. He wrote his daughter Ellen from Milwaukee in February to say that he had "awed my Wisconsin senate [for all the legislature was at Madison] with a richer orotund than they had heard" because he had caught cold in Chicago, and had taken time to look "through all the halls of the University & the Historical Society under friendly guidance." During this lecture tour he wrote almost constantly to his daughters, Ellen and Edith, and less to anyone else.

Back in Concord, he reflected more and more on age, 137

though he was not yet sixty. "One capital advantage of old age is the absolute insignificance of a success more or less. Thirty years ago it had really been a matter of importance to me whether [a lecture] was good and effective. Now it is none in relation to me. It is long already fixed what I can and what I cannot do." Old men, he wrote in his journal, "are drunk with time," but "In youth, the day is not long enough."

He acknowledged himself a member of the new Republican party, one for reform of slavery, which, by declaring itself forthrightly for abolition, had attracted to it all the dissident members of the other political parties of the time. In 1860 he supported Lincoln and cast his vote for him. He looked upon Lincoln's election as "sublime, the pronunciation of the masses of America against Slavery."

All during that year, however, Emerson had been busy preparing a new book. It consisted of a revision of lectures he had given under the general title of the book, *The Conduct of Life,* and it was published December 8, 1860. Readers looked in vain for any chapter on slavery or abolition or even on political matters which were then the topics of the day. There was no controversy in it at all, yet there was everywhere in American life controversy of so grievous a nature that the country stood divided on the threshold of war.

Here were the once popular essays, designed to guide the reader through life—*Wealth, Power, Beauty, Worship* and others. The theme of compensation made its appearance once more in *Power;* belief in it "must control every effort that is made by an industrious one." Self-reliance was still—as always—the key to satisfactory living. "The basis of good manners is self-reliance," he wrote in *Behavior.* "Necessity is the law of all who are not self-possessed. Those who are not self-possessed obtrude and pain us. Some men appear to feel that they belong to a Pariah caste. They fear to offend, they bend and apologize, and walk through life with a timid step. . . . A person of strong mind comes to perceive that for him immunity is secured so long as he renders to society that service which is native and proper to him,—an immunity from all the observances, yea, and duties, which society so tyrannically imposes on the rank and file of its members."

He paid tribute anew to Nature. "The permanent interest of every man is, never to be in a false position," he set forth in *Illusions,* but "to have the weight of Nature to back him in all that he does. Riches and poverty are a thick or thin costume; and our life—the life of all of us—identical. For we transcend the circumstance continually, and taste the real quality of existence, as in our employments, which only differ in the manipulations, but express the same laws; or in our thoughts, which wear no silks and taste no ice-creams."

Conduct of Life sounded all the notes and themes that had come to be identified with him. There was a notable absence of any evidence in it, as in its predecessors, that he had a theory of evil; and the absence of such a theory accounted in large part for the optimism that informed all his writing. Man, in his opinion, was superior to the view he held of himself, and he expected that Americans ought to know it or would come to recognize it. He scored intellectual laziness, the lack of awareness—far too many of his neighbors walked through Nature unseeing, and his sense of expectancy, arising from his optimism, invariably shone through everything he wrote. What he had to say in *Conduct of Life,* as in his earlier books, rose from his identification with the core of the American character and a more intimate acquaintance with the American experience than his critics gave him credit for. What he had to say transcended the agony of the looming Civil War.

God offers to every mind its choice between truth and repose. Take which you please,— you can never have both. Between these, as a pendulum, man oscillates. He in whom the love of repose predominates will accept the first creed, the first philosophy, the first political party he meets,—most likely his father's. He gets rest, commodity and reputation; but he shuts the door to truth. He in whom the love of truth predominates will keep himself aloof from all moorings, and afloat. He will abstain from dogmatism, and recognize all the opposite negations between which, as walls, his being is swung. He submits to the inconvenience of suspense and imperfect opinion, but he is a candidate for truth, as the other is not, and respects the highest law of his being.

Intellect

The war enlisted him to the extent of his limitations. Though he began the lecture series of 1861 with his customary subjects, he was soon adding new lectures —Civilization at a Pinch, American Nationality, and others, adapted to the need of the times. He contributed money and time when he was called upon to do so, and managed to get muskets for his son Edward's drill club. As the year turned, he was in Washington, where he lectured at the Smithsonian Institution, visiting Charles Sumner, and through him, cabinet officers and President Abraham Lincoln, who reminded Emerson that he had once heard him speak and say "that a Kentuckian seems to say by his air and manners, 'Here am I; if you don't like me, the worse for you.' "

He made more entries in his journal than he had done in the immediately previous years, still facing his world on his terms, still searching for truth, still optimistic in spite of the shock of the Battle of Bull Run which made it clear to him as to other northerners that the war was not to be of short duration or easily won. "Hitch your wagon to a star," he wrote. "Do the like in your choice of tasks. Let us not fag in paltry selfish tasks which aim at private benefit alone. No god will help. . . . Let us work rather for those interests which the gods honour and promote: justice, love, utility, freedom, knowledge."

CHAPTER 11

The Years of Decline

He continued to pay tribute to Nature: "When I bought my farm, I did not know what a bargain I had in the bluebirds, bobolinks, and thrushes; as little did I know what sublime mornings and sunsets I was buying." And of his craft he wrote, "The art of the writer is to speak his fact and have done. Let the reader find that he cannot afford to omit any line of your writing, because you have omitted every word that he can spare."

He scored an increasing concern in his fellow men with the opinions of others. "As people rise in the social scale, they think more of each other's opinion than of their own. And 't is hard to find one who does not measure his business and daily performance from the supposed estimate. And yet, his own is the only standard. Down in the pits of hunger and want life has a real dignity, from this doing the best, instead of the seemly. The sailor on the topmast in a storm, the hunter amidst the snowdrifts, the woodman in the depth of the forest, cannot stop to think how he looks, or what London or Paris would say, and therefore his garb and behaviour have a certain dignity, like the works of Nature around him; he would as soon ask what the crows and muskrats think of him."

Time was taking toll of his friends. Hawthorne's health was worsening. In England Arthur Clough died. And Thoreau, who had gone to Minnesota in a vain hope of improving his tubercular condition, died of that scourge on May 6, 1862. Emerson delivered the funeral oration. "The country knows not yet, or in the least part," he said prophetically, "how great a son it has lost. It seems an injury that he should leave in the midst his broken task which none else can finish, a kind of indignity to so noble a soul that he should depart out of Nature before he has been really shown to his peers for what he is. But he, at least, is content. His soul was made for the noblest society; he had in a short life exhausted the capabilities of this world; wherever there is knowledge, wherever there is virtue, wherever there is beauty, he will find a home."

Thoreau's death grieved and troubled him. "Henry Thoreau remains erect, calm, self-subsistent, before me," he wrote in his journal, ". . . but he is not long out of mind when I walk, and, as today, row upon the pond. He chose wisely no doubt for himself to be the bachelor of thought and nature that he was,—how near to the old monks in their ascetic religion! He had no talent for wealth, and knew how to be poor without the least hint of squalor or inelegance. Perhaps he fell—all of us do—into his way of living, without forecasting it much, but approved and confirmed it with later wisdom."

Reading Thoreau's journal a year later, he admitted that he was "very sensible of the vigour of his constitution. That oaken strength which I noted whenever he walked, or worked, or surveyed woodlots . . . Henry shows in his literary task. He has muscle, and ventures on and performs feats which I am forced to decline. In reading him, I find the same thought, the same spirit that is in me, but he takes a step beyond, and illustrates by excellent images that which I should have conveyed in a sleepy generality."

To celebrate the Emancipation Proclamation, Emerson wrote the poem *Boston Hymn* for a jubilee held in Boston on the first of January, 1863. Later, he spoke in support of Robert Gould Shaw's Negro regiment and made a donation to the regiment fund. Still later, he joined the Union Club in Boston.

Events now crowded upon him. Aunt Mary Moody Emerson died at the age of eighty-eight on May 1, 1863. He was, much to his surprise, appointed to the Committee of Visitation to West Point. He met John Burroughs, the young naturalist then teaching not far from West Point, and the pop-

143

ular humorist, Donald Mitchell, who wrote under the name of Ik Marvel. He lectured at Dartmouth and Waterville colleges, criticizing England for its sympathy for the South. He wrote a dirge for Colonel Shaw and his Negro regiment. He prepared a new lecture titled *The Fortune of the Republic,* indicting England anew, and vaunting his faith in and hope for the Republic. He used his influence on behalf of Walt Whitman in Washington, helping to get him a job there.

Toward the end of 1863 he was reflecting in his journal that "people only see what they are prepared to see. Thus, who sees birds, except the hunter, or the ornithologist?" A few months later, in 1864, he lamented his failing powers in the pages of his journal. "The grief of old age is, that now, only in rare moments, and by happiest combinations or consent of the elements, can we attain those enlargements and that inellectual *élan,* which were once a daily gift." But he added that "old age brings along with its ugliness the comfort that you will soon be out of it," though he was now but sixty-one.

In 1864 he was elected to the American Academy of Arts and Sciences, and that winter he inaugurated a new series of lectures entitled *American Life* in Boston, and thereafter tried in the course of the winter of 1864–65 to satisfy the many requests for his lectures that came in, going as far west as Chicago and Milwaukee, where he lived in "the best hotels," and complained a little of his "weak stomach."

When Hawthorne died in 1864, he was left with Alcott and Ellery Channing as walking companions. Of Hawthorne, he wrote after the funeral on a day of "pomp of sunshine and verdure, and gentle winds," that it "was easy to talk with him,—there were no barriers,—only, he said so little, that I talked too much, and stopped only because, as he gave no indications, I feared to exceed. He showed no egotism or self-assertion, rather a humility, and, at one time, a fear that he had written himself out." Of Channing he set down in his journal that one "must carry a stenographic press in your pocket to save his commentaries on things and men, or they are irrecoverable" because Channing's genius was all an "Incessant whirl."

The assassination of Lincoln was the occasion for his preparation of a eulogy for the slain President delivered on the day of the funeral services at a memorial in Concord meeting house. "This man grew according to the need. His mind mastered the problem of the day; and as the problem grew, so did his comprehension of it. Rarely was man so fitted to the event. . . . There is a serene Providence which . . . makes its own instruments, creates the man of the time, trains him in poverty, inspires his genius, and arms him for his task."

But he was writing considerably less. When George William Childs of the Philadelphia *Public Ledger* asked him in June, 1865, to make a contribution to his paper, Emerson replied, "I rarely write, & usually feel that the *Atlantic Monthly* has a first claim to any papers of mine."

After his daughter Edith's wedding to William Forbes in October, he found it necessary to plan yet another season of lecturing. "This juvenile career," he had called it the previous February—but the budget demanded the income he received from lectures, though his new son-in-law was soon making judicious investments for him, and earning more money for Emerson. The winters of 1865–66 and 1866–67 took him again as far west as the Mississippi valley.

Between the two tours he received the honorary degree of Doctor of Laws from Harvard and became a grandfather for the first time, on the birth of Edith's son, Ralph Emerson Forbes. With a party of friends he climbed Mt. Monadnock. "We look down . . . on a hundred farms and farmhouses, but never see horse or man. . . . Around us the arctic sparrow, *Fringilla nivalis,* flies and peeps, the ground-robin also; but you can hear the distant song of the wood-thrushes ascending from the green belts below." On another occasion, with Lidian and Ellen, he spent the day with Agassiz at his house and on the Nahant rocks. "He is a man to be thankful for, always cordial, full of facts, with unsleeping observation, and perfectly communicative." On the day of his visit he recorded in his journal that he found his "biography in every fable that I read."

On his return from his winter tour in 1867, he began to prepare the manuscript of a new collection of poems, revising and polishing. "The just pride of a man consists herein," he wrote at this time, "that the recognition of him by others is no wise necessary to him."

May-day and Other Pieces was published late in April. It contained all the poems Emerson wished to preserve among those he had written since his first collection twenty years before. For all that he had written many verses as a young man, he had not been prolific as a poet; the volume was spare, though it contained poems which had already been widely printed and were well-known to many readers. One of its poems, *Terminus,* revealed his acceptance of the limitations of age:

> It is time to be old,
> To take in sail:—
> The god of bounds,
> Who sets to seas a shore,
> Came to me in his fatal rounds,
> And said: "No more!
> No farther shoot
> Thy broad ambitious branches, and thy root.

> Fancy departs: no more invent;
> Contract thy firmament
> To compass of a tent. . . ."

There was no lessening of Emerson's direction away from traditional forms, and, though there was nothing conservative in his attitudes, there was also nothing in the substance of his preaching to the effect that poets ought to write about the events of the day, opposing war, vaunting freedom and laws for the good of all, hailing universal suffrage, and the like. The title poem celebrated the delights of nature; it rose from the same well as his journal entry of 1868: "The only place where I feel the joy of eminent domain is in my woodlot. My spirits rise whenever I enter it. I can spend the entire day there with hatchet or pruning-shears making paths, without a remorse of wasting time. I fancy the birds know me, and even the trees make little speeches or hint them." The majority of the other poems reflected familiar themes or restated them.

Next spring his daughter Ellen traveled with him ever more frequently. In Brooklyn that season they went to hear Henry Ward Beecher, whose orthodoxy no more shook Emerson's lack of it than Lidian's attempts to bring him back into the fold; on their way from the church they found themselves in a crowd of people and caught sight of General Ulysses Grant. His Brooklyn lectures were complicated by ill health, but he was not daunted by it.

In September he was shaken by his brother William's death, soon after that of William's widow, Susan Haven Emerson. His death was a grievous blow to Emerson; they had carried on a lifelong correspondence, and William was the last of his brothers. Writing to the poet Emma Lazarus of the event, he added: "To the poet every month & every day is the best of the year, & though the activity & the use is less, I do not know that the sensibility to Nature diminishes with age"— testifying to the comfort he sought and found in nature to assuage any wound.

"A man never gets acquainted with himself, but is always a surprise," he noted in his journal as 1868 drew to a close. His preoccupations were never far from him. "Religions," he wrote not long afterward, "are the amusements of the intellect." But he was not given to any "foolish consistency," for, though he had been dubious about woman's suffrage as late as 1867, in 1869 he made it clear in an address to the New England Woman Suffrage Association that he now believed the movement was right. As an overseer of Harvard University, he supported reform and voted with the majority for Charles Eliot as Harvard's new president.

During most of 1869 he was at work preparing the manuscript of a new book of essays. This was *Society and Solitude*. By October the early chapters of the manuscript were ready for the printer; by 1870 it appeared in print, sounding all the familiar Emersonian notes. But most of the essays in this book had been familiar lectures a decade before.

Here again were self-reliance, compensation, Nature. In *Farming* he celebrated the farmer who "times himself to Nature, and acquires that livelong patience which belongs to her" and Nature's method of *"all for each and each for all."* In the title essay he declared that "no man is fit to society who has fine traits," however he might be admired at a distance, but the remedy lay in "habits of self-reliance that should go in practice to making the man independent of the human race, or else a religion of love."

The book sold well. Emerson was now held to be the most distinguished writer living in America, and in the spring of 1870 he was lecturing in philosophy at Harvard, though teaching even in this form was still unattractive to him. Carlyle, having read *Society and Solitude,* praised its virtues—which were the same virtues already evident in the first *Essays,* but cavilled at Emerson's failure to recognize evil, charging that Emerson took "so little heed of the frightful quantities of friction and perverse impediment there everywhere are."

Emerson was not impressed—however gratified he might have been—by the sales of *Society and Solitude.* "My new book," he set forth in his journal in March, 1870, "sells faster . . . than either of its foregoers. This is not for its merit, but only shows that old age is a good advertisement. Your name has been seen so often that your book must be worth buying."

He was now approaching his sixty-seventh birthday, and he was glad to give up his Harvard lecturing in favor of a Pullman journey to the west coast at the invitation of John M. Forbes, his daughter Edith's father-in-law. He lectured in California, visited Yosemite, met Bret Harte and the naturalist John Muir, who pressed him to go hiking with him in the Sierras. He was impressed with the country "everywhere rich in trees & endless flowers" and with the "awe & terror lying over this new garden—all empty as yet of any adequate people, yet with this assured future in American hands,—unequalled in climate and production."

However exhilarated he was by his journey, he was happy to be home again.

*The best part of truth is certainly that
which hovers in gleams and suggestions
unpossessed before man. His recorded
knowledge is dead and cold. But this chorus
of thoughts and hopes, these dawning truths,
like great stars just lifting themselves into
his horizon, they are his future, and console
him for the ridiculous brevity and meanness
of his civic life.*
     The Journals of Ralph Waldo Emerson

Despite the fact that his memory was now failing him, and that he was much given to repetition in his lectures, he set about preparing for another winter of lecturing. Bret Harte came east and visited him in Concord, but Harte was too rough a stone for Emerson's polishing.

Emerson went out on tour once more, again to the Mississippi valley, as far as Iowa. He came back to lecture in Baltimore and Washington, where he visited Charles Sumner and at Harvard University gave a lecture entitled *What Books to Read.* At Concord, soon after, he read his lecture *Immortality.* By mid-April, 1872, he delivered half a dozen informal "conversations" at Mechanics' Hall in Boston, but these were not entirely successful, for they were not as well put together as his earlier lectures had been.

He was sharply aware of his increasing shortcomings. On May 26, 1872, he wrote in his journal, "Yesterday, my sixty-ninth birthday, I found myself on my round of errands in Summer Street, and, though close on the spot where I was born, was looking into a street with some bewilderment and read on the sign *Kingston Street,* with surprise, finding in the granite blocks no hint of Nathaniel Goddard's pasture and long wooden fence, and so of my nearness to my native

CHAPTER 12

"A Rendering-up of Responsibility"

corner of Chauncy Place." But his concern with religion did not subside. "One thing is certain," he confined to his journal, "the religions are obsolete when the reforms do not proceed from them."

Late in July of that year the Emerson house caught fire. The sound of the flames woke him. He found the garret full of smoke, and, after waking Lidian, ran outside to shout to his neighbors, who in turn roused the village. His townsmen turned out to save whatever could be taken from the house, and the local firemen attacked the fire with enough vigor to save much of the house. Alcott's daughters, Louisa May and her sister, Mary, took charge of manuscripts that were brought out. "The whole town came to our help & never were household goods from least to largest so tenderly removed & cared for," he wrote John Murray Forbes on July 26, in response to a telegram.

When the news of the fire was spread, the response of his friends was overwhelming. Though his insurance would cover repair of the house, offers of $5,000 came from Caroline Sturgis Tappan and Francis Lowell, who brought that sum as a gift from friends. Judge Ebenezer Hoar opened his bank account to Emerson, who had removed his books to a room in the court house, though the family took up quarters in the Old Manse until the house could be repaired.

The shock of the fire took its toll and the decline in his health alarmed his family and friends. He spoke about the disposal of his manuscripts, and voiced his regret that essays and sketches he meant to write would now not be written. He was persuaded to relax at Naushon Island, where on August 31 he noted in his journal, "I thought today, in these rare seaside woods, that if absolute leisure were offered me, I should run to the college or the scientific school which offered best lectures on geology, chemistry, minerals, botany, and seek to make the alphabets of these sciences clear to me. How could leisure or labour be better employed?"

He was now in his seventieth year and Ellen took it upon herself to seek advice from Dr. Edward Clarke, pointing out to him that Emerson's memory had begun to fail half a decade before, and had grown steadily worse, that his work had become difficult for him, that what he said and wrote was now quite repetitive. He said one day, after looking at some proofs, "I get the impression in reading them that they talk too much about the same thing, but I cannot find out." A trip abroad seemed to be indicated.

By mid-October the contributions of friends came to just under twenty thousand dollars and Emerson was refusing to accept anything more. Offers of aid had come from abroad as well as from his friends at home. That month he went to New York to speak briefly at a banquet in honor of Froude, now in America on a lecture tour. On October 23, he and Ellen left New York on the *Wyoming;* on November 3 they reached Liverpool, and next day met Edward Emerson, then in England.

They went to London, saw Carlyle and some other friends, went on to Paris, Avignon, Marseilles—then into Italy, to Florence, Rome, Naples—but their destination was Egypt. On Christmas Day they reached Alexandria, and in January they were in Cairo, staying at Shepheard's Hotel. Emerson was impressed with the "erect carriage . . . of the Copts . . . better and nobler in figure and movement than any passengers in our cities at home."

They went up the Nile, visiting Thebes and Luxor. He wrote Lidian from Thebes, "We enjoy heartily this watery journey, & have spent the last two days in the colossal temples on the two sides of the river here. Every day is clear & hot, the sky rich, the shores lined with palm groves, the birds innumera-

153

ble, the ibis, the penguin, the hawk & the eagle, with vast flights of geese & ducks & flocks of little birds of sparrow size who fly in a rolling globe, whirl round & return again every minute. . . . The Nile has daily the appearance of a long lake whose end we are always fast approaching. . . ."

He enjoyed traveling, and noted later in his journal that its enjoyment lay in "the arrival at a new city . . . the feeling of free adventure, you have no duties,—nobody knows you, nobody has claims, you are like a boy on his first visit to the Common on Election Day. . . . For the first time for many years you wake master of the bright day, in a bright world without a claim on you; only leave to enjoy."

From Philae they turned back, retracing their journey. Emerson met an early disciple in George Owen; in Rome young Henry James came to visit, and so did Elizabeth Hoar, William Wetmore Story, the artist, and others; in Florence he saw Bayard Taylor; in Paris, Ivan Turgenev, Ernest Renan, Hippolyte Taine. By early April they were again in London, where he saw Robert Browning, Charles Reade, Froude—home from his American tour—Max Müller, William Gladstone, and Thomas Henry Huxley, and at Oxford, John Ruskin and Benjamin Jowett.

In late May, 1873, they returned home to a festive celebration arranged by the village of Concord, the townsmen of which were summoned to the station by the constant whistling of the engine on the train bearing Emerson and Ellen, beginning at Walden so that everyone would have time to reach the station before the train pulled in.

The Emerson house had now been restored and Emerson settled down to the domestic life to which he had grown accustomed. His lecture tours were now done if his lecturing was not. In October he gave the address on the occasion of the opening of the Concord Free Public Library; in May, 1874, he delivered an address in the chapel of the Harvard Divinity School; and he appeared on occasion at the Concord Lyceum, where in 1875 he lectured on oratory. In that same year he delivered the centennial address at the unveiling of Daniel Chester French's *Minute Man* and spoke in Philadelphia, where he was paid for a single lecture as much as a season's tour had once brought him.

He looked forward to another book of his essays, but it was no longer possible for him to revise and polish, and he accepted the help of Ellen and of James Elliott Cabot. *Letters and Social Aims* was published in December, 1875. Late the following year, the volume *Selected Poems* made its appearance; he had lent more of a hand to its preparation than to that of its predecessor, but it had come into being again because of the work of Ellen and Cabot.

Many honors now came to him from every quarter, but fame meant no more to him than it ever had. Books were dedicated to him; Concord proposed to name a street after him but he persuaded the village fathers to name it Thoreau Street instead; in 1878 he was made a member of the Institut de France; he sat for his bust to Daniel Chester French; he bore the adulation of many who came to pay homage to him.

When, after the death of Thomas Carlyle, the Massachusetts Historical Society invited him to speak about Carlyle, he found himself unable to prepare an address but appeared before that body in February, 1881, to read a paper he had taken largely from a letter written in 1848, after his second visit with Carlyle.

His existence now was a retiring one, though he still on occasion attended meetings of the Saturday Club. Now and then he saw visitors: Bronson Alcott and Louisa May, Walt Whitman—who came to sit with Emerson, though few words passed between them—the young Edward Bok, Mary Baker

Eddy—who came with the intention of bringing him back to the faith but retreated in defeat.

He continued to take walks whenever he felt well enough. He attended the funerals of Charles Sumner and Henry Wadsworth Longfellow, and in his last year took a brief holiday at Naushon Island. In February, 1882, he waded through the snowdrifts to hear F. B. Sanborn read from his life of Thoreau, soon to be published. Still later, he was present at a meeting of the Concord Social Circle. On the second of April he and Ellen walked to Walden, still one of his favorite walks.

He took cold, but insisted on walking throughout that April until pneumonia forced him to keep to his bed. He was up and about in his room almost to his last hour. He spoke of his dead son, Waldo—"that beautiful boy"—to Lidian. He invited Ellery Channing to come again to dine, as he had done so often. He sat by the fire for a while on his last day, April 27, 1882. At ten minutes to nine that evening he died. He would have been seventy-nine in less than a month.

Over a thousand people came to Concord for the funeral on the thirtieth of April. A private ceremony was conducted by William Furness. This was followed by a service at the Unitarian Church, where James Clarke gave the address and Bronson Alcott read a sonnet to Emerson, celebrating earlier days. He was buried in Sleepy Hollow Cemetery, not far from the graves of Hawthorne and Thoreau. The long search for truth was over at last.

He never faltered, never compromised; the prophet of the ideal faced the real and told the truth about it, serenely and with clear insight. . . . A friend of civilization, he was partisan only to the ideal; to justice, truth, righteousness. . . . A free soul, he was the flowering of two centuries of spiritual aspiration.

Vernon L. Parrington
Main Currents in American Thought

Though for the decade preceding his death, Ralph Waldo Emerson had written little, he was at the time of his death looked upon as America's foremost writer, spiritual leader, and philosopher. A two-volume edition of his *Prose Works,* the revision of which he had undertaken, had appeared in 1870; *The Complete Works of Ralph Waldo Emerson,* edited by Edward W. Emerson, appeared in 1903—4, followed by the *Journals of Ralph Waldo Emerson,* edited by Edward W. Emerson and W. E. Forbes, from 1909 to 1914. The principal writings of Emerson have never been out of print since his death.

The first biography of Emerson made its appearance a year before his death in George W. Cooke's *Ralph Waldo Emerson: His Life, Writings, and Philosophy.* James Eliot Cabot's *A Memoir of Ralph Waldo Emerson* followed in 1887. George Woodberry's *Ralph Waldo Emerson* (1907) remains perhaps the most adequate brief biography, but the definitive biography did not appear until 1949, in *The Life of Ralph Waldo Emerson,* by Ralph L. Rusk. Scores of studies and interpretations have appeared in print throughout the twentieth century, and George W. Cooke's early *A Bibliography of Ralph Waldo Emerson* (1908) is today but a beginning, and must be considered inadequate by present standards.

Afterword

Emerson was a product of his age. He reflected the idealism that prevailed in the nineteenth century, and its optimism informed all his insights. But he **was as** careful as an artist as he was reserved as a man. He thought of himself as a "born poet, of a low class no doubt, but a poet," but for all his study of classical models his poetry led away from traditional forms to verse that most of his contemporaries thought awkward, but which took root rather in the English metaphysical poets of the seventeenth century, and which, through its disregard for metrics and its vaunting of the symbol as an instrument of expression, led directly to modern poetry, from Hart Crane and T. S. Eliot to Wallace Stevens and e. e. cummings, for which Walt Whitman is commonly but mistakenly given credit.

In his lifelong pursuit of truth he soon recognized the chasm between the ideal and reality and strove to bridge it. Early he grew aware of the incompatibility between the moral law and the natural law and sought some accommodation between them. Like Thoreau and most of his fellow Transcendentalists he looked to the self-reliant individual to effect some compromise between the growing materialism of American civilization and the ideal of freedom forever in man's dreams. He was disturbingly cognizant of the impending machine technology of the twentieth century, and may have foreseen the inevitability of man's destruction, again, of his earthly paradise.

In his individualism, his self-reliance, his idealism as well as in his optimism, Emerson was closer to the heart of the American character than any other writer of his time. The experience of reading Emerson remains a profitable one for any age, but particularly for youth. J. Donald Adams puts it

effectively in his introduction to the *Poems of Ralph Waldo*

Emerson (1965), when he writes that the early reading of Emerson made easier for him "some of the most difficult decisions" he had to make in life because Emerson fortifies "the will to make the best and most of life."

Bibliographical Notes

The reader who wishes to read Emerson or to learn more about him and his work will find certain books outstanding. The Centenary Edition of *The Complete Works of Ralph Waldo Emerson*, edited by Edward Waldo Emerson, in twelve volumes (Boston: Houghton Mifflin Company, 1903–4) is, of course, standard. This should be supplemented with *The Journals of Ralph Waldo Emerson*, edited by Edward Waldo Emerson and Waldo Emerson Forbes, in ten volumes (Boston: Houghton Mifflin Company, 1909–14), though the scholar will prefer *The Journals and Miscellaneous Notebooks of Ralph Waldo Emerson*, edited by William H. Gilman and others (Cambridge: The Belknap Press of Harvard University Press, 1961–   ), and *The Letters of Ralph Waldo Emerson*, edited by Ralph L. Rusk in six volumes (New York: Columbia University Press, 1939). Hitherto uncollected work is available in *The Early Lectures of Ralph Waldo Emerson*, edited by Stephen E. Whicher and Robert E. Spiller, Volume I, 1959; Volume II, with Wallace E. Williams, 1963 (Cambridge: Harvard University Press), and *Young Emerson Speaks*, the sermons edited by Arthur C. McGiffert, Jr. (Boston: Houghton Mifflin Company, 1938).

There are various selective volumes available which will serve the reader as effectively if not comprehensively. Perhaps the best of these is *The Complete Essays and Other Writings of Ralph Waldo Emerson*, edited in one volume with a biographical introduction by Brooks Atkinson (New York: Random House, Modern Library, 1940). This can be supplemented with *The Portable Emerson*, edited and with an introduction by Mark Van Doren (New York: The Viking Press, 1946). Other selections of value to the student are *Selected*

Writings of Ralph Waldo Emerson, edited and with a fore-word by William H. Gilman (New York: New American Library, 1965); *Selected Essays, Lectures, and Poems of Ralph Waldo Emerson*, edited and with an introduction by Robert E. Spiller (New York: Washington Square Press, Pocket Books, 1965), and *Essays and Poems of Ralph Waldo Emerson*, selected and arranged by G. F. Maine, with an introduction by DeLancey Ferguson (London: Collins, 1954).

A good selection of the *Poems of Ralph Waldo Emerson* by J. Donald Adams is available (New York: Thomas Y. Crowell Company, 1965). The journals can best be sampled in *The Heart of Emerson's Journals*, edited by Bliss Perry (Boston: Houghton Mifflin Company, 1909) and in *The Journals of Ralph Waldo Emerson*, selected and edited by Robert N. Linscott (New York: Random House, Modern Library, 1960).

The most complete biography is certainly Ralph L. Rusk's *The Life of Ralph Waldo Emerson* (New York: Columbia University Press, 1949), though many other biographies, from the early two-volume *Memoir* by Emerson's friend James Elliot Cabot to Van Wyck Brooks's *The Life of Emerson* (New York: E. P. Dutton & Company, 1932) offer insights. For a view of Emerson in literary perspective see *Literary History of the United States*, edited by Robert E. Spiller, Willard Thorp, Thomas H. Johnson, Henry Seidel Canby and Associates (New York: The Macmillan Company, 1948) and Van Wyck Brooks's *The Flowering of New England* (New York: E. P. Dutton & Company, 1936) and *New England: Indian Summer* (New York: E. P. Dutton & Company, 1940).

An interesting and challenging contemporary evaluation of Emerson's influence on American poets and poetry is to be found in Hyatt H. Waggoner's *American Poets from the Puritans to the Present* (Boston: Houghton Mifflin Company, 1968). The student interested in Emerson's growth as an essayist seen in a contemporary reinterpretation of a single essay will find *Emerson's 'Nature': Origin, Growth, Meaning,* edited by Merton M. Sealts, Jr. and Alfred R. Ferguson (New York: Dodd, Mead & Company, 1969) indispensable. While there is no really adequate critical estimate of Emerson, there are many books of value to the student. Among them are Sherman Paul's *Emerson's Angle of Vision* (Cambridge: Harvard University Press, 1952); Vivian C. Hopkins's *Spires of Form: A Study of Emerson's Aesthetic Theory* (Cambridge: Harvard University Press, 1951); and Stephen E. Whicher's *Freedom and Fate: An Inner Life of Ralph Waldo Emerson* (Philadelphia: University of Philadelphia Press, 1953). Finally, Joel Porte's *Emerson and Thoreau: Transcendentalists in Conflict* (Middletown, Conn.: Wesleyan University Press, 1966) is a brilliantly reasoned comparison of the thinking of Emerson and Thoreau.

INDEX